Gaelic Football Training Drills

By: Mike Culloty & Pat O'Shea

© 1994
Printed by: Kingdom Printers Ltd, Tralee (066) 21136
Published by: COS Productions
Tralee, Co. Kerry, Ireland • Phone: (066) 26562 Fax: (066) 23882

About the Authors

MICHAEL CULLOTY is a native of Tralee where he played football with the Austin Stacks G.A.A. Club. He has represented his county at minor and under 21 levels. He obtained his Bachelor Education Degree in Physical Education in 1976 at Thomond College, Limerick. He has worked as a physical education teacher and coach in St. Mary's Secondary School, Moyderwell, Tralee since 1979. He has coached teams in all grades at school and club level and is a regular contributor at coaching courses. In 1991 he was seconded from the Department of Education to the position of G.A.A. Field Officer in Munster, a position in which he has seen extensive involvement in all Coaching and Games Development initiatives throughout the Province. He is married with three children and lives at Listellick, near Tralee.

PAT O'SHEA is a native of Killarney where he plays his football with the Dr. Crokes G.A.A. Club. Recognised as the most lethal corner forward at club level in the Kingdom, he played a starring role in his club's march to The All Ireland Club Title in 1992. He obtained his Diploma in Recreation and Leisure Management at Waterford Regional College in 1987. In 1989 he was appointed by the Munster Council and the Kerry County Board as football coach in the county. As coach he is heavily involved in the development of players at primary level and organises summer camps, coaching clinics and courses at club level. He has coached the Kerry Vocational Schools team to All Ireland success in 1990. He is married with one child and lives in Killarney.

Table of Contents

Acknowledgments

We wish to acknowledge the contributions of the following to this publication:

- Margaret and Deborah Ann, who provided constant support and survived many hours of debate on football and drills.

The Generous financial contribution of:
- Mr Bill Kennedy, Manager, Lee Strand Co-Operative Creamery Ltd., Tralee.

- John Quirke, Quirke's Sand and Gravel Ltd., Killorglan

- Bill and Mary Kirby, Kirby's Brogue Inn and Steakhouse, Rock St., Tralee

- Hennebery's Sports Centre Ltd., Ashe St., Tralee

- John & Kayrena, Dowling Sports, Bridge St., Tralee

- Chris Reina, David Keane, Bernie Keane and the staff at Kingdom Printers Ltd., Tralee whose expertise, support and guidance was always friendly and truly professional.

- Our friends who encouraged us to persevere.

- Our God, "...for with God all things are possible." Mark 10:27.

Introduction

BASED ON OUR EXPERIENCES with coaches and players at all levels of Gaelic Football over the past three years it may be said that there are some features which are becoming increasingly evident:

- There is a perception that standards are dropping.

- There is an over emphasis on physical fitness at most, if not all, levels.

- There is a decrease in the actual time allocated to skill training and improvement.

- Players do not practice as much on their own as heretofore.

- Consequently the need for well organised training sessions, which adequately cater for both the skill and tactical elements of the game, assumes ever increasing importance.

- Coaches are more aware of these features than anyone else and are constantly seeking new ideas and methods which will improve practices and skill levels among their players.

- There is a clear and distinct demand for training drills among coaches at all levels.

THIS PUBLICATION attempts to address that demand by producing a book on Gaelic Football based solely on training drills which , sadly, to date has been neglected in the print media generally. It is our response to the innumerable requests we have received "in the field" for training drills. Our chief objectives are that the many drills presented here will help to enhance the confidence of our coaches, improve skill levels and playing standards and increase the enjoyment of our games for both coaches and players. It is hoped that the book will become an indispensable part of the coaches "kit bag" – it is not meant for the shelf! – an ever ready and easy to use planner for any and every training session. If we achieve some reasonable progress towards the achievement of these objectives we will have been very satisfied with our work.

FINALLY, WE WOULD ENCOURAGE coaches everywhere to share their thoughts, methods, drills and ideas on the game with each other. Every single coach has a contribution to make to the betterment of Gaelic Football for the player, the coach and the spectator. There are thousands of more drills and ideas because there are thousands of more coaches and players. Perhaps a suitable forum, focussing solely on the game, could be organised where coaches everywhere would be given the opportunity to contribute and where this immense pool of knowledge could be shared, explored, added to and drawn from. Such a forum would be most welcome in our view and of tremendous benefit to all involved in the game.

IN THE MEANTIME we wish you continued enjoyment and success in your coaching and trust that you will find this book to be a helpful and worthwhile investment.

Guidelines and general points on the use of drills.

1. WHY DRILLS SHOULD FORM AN INTEGRAL PART OF YOUR TRAINING SESSION:

- **"PRACTICE MAKES PERFECT"** is on old adage but remains as true as ever today. It is now widely recognised that repetition of a particular movement or skill is perhaps the most critical element in skill develoment. Simply stated, by repeating a skill many times in practice, the skill is eventually performed automatically, smoothly and effortlessly. Think of any of the 'great' players in our game and you will agree that this is their trademark!

- **BY USING DRILLS,** for example any of the kicking drills, it is possible to have a player kicking the ball over 100 times, on both sides of his/her body, in the space of just five minutes. This will be true for every player in the drill, not just one or two. This type of practice, using the many different drills as suggested throughout the book, will have a tremendous effect on player and skill development and improvement, even in the short space of a few weeks.

- **THE CONTRAST BETWEEN** this activity and what is sometimes witnessed in a 20 or 30 minute game situation, where some players may catch and kick a ball on only three or four occasions is obvious. Improving as a player requires more and a well organised drill section in your session will ensure that in the real game situation the player who may get the ball only once or twice will automatically perform the necessary skills in those situations.

- **EVERY TRAINING SESSION** should include a drill section, with you as coach deciding on the skills to be improved – catching; kicking; passing, etc, and on the drills to be used. Don't despair if everything fails to run like a dream on a new drill. Players will need to get used to the drill and in no time at all they will be enjoying themselves no end! And, of course, practicing, practicing, practicing!

2. POINTS TO REMEMBER:

- **IN THE BOOK, EACH SKILL,** e.g. kicking, soloing, etc., has its own drill section.

- **EACH DRILL SECTION IS GRADED,** with the "easier" drills appearing early on and progressively increasing in difficulty towards the end of the section.

- **EACH DRILL SECTION** should not be confined to that skill alone however. For example, every handpass drill and kicking drill are automatically catching drills. Every handpass drill may be used as a kicking drill by increasing the distance between stations. Some goalkeeping drills may be used as shooting drills, and so on. As an example, examine Drill 11 in the Handpass Section and Catching Drill 7. Same drill with different emphasis. Compare with Kicking Drill 8 where, with a slight variation, it becomes a kick and handpass drill. See the possibilities. Try them out. Your players will be delighted with you!!

- **PLAYERS SHOULD BE ENCOURAGED** to use both sides of their body - left foot, right foot, left hand, right hand. Drills can be used to work exclusively on one side, e.g. the weak side, or on alternate sides in the same drill. On occasion this can be achieved quite simply by reversing the direction of player movement.

- **WHILE MANY OF THE DRILLS** in the book include variations it is advisable for you as a coach to always be looking for ways of adding to or improving any particular drill.

3. GETTING STARTED : WHAT YOU NEED

- **SMALL CONES OR FLAGS** are needed to mark out the drill stations. Where these are not available, tracksuit tops or jerseys may be used. Making use of existing pitch markings, 13m, 20m, and 45m lines, sidelines and endlines gives many advantages when laying down cones.

- **FOOTBALLS:** Always have as many footballs as possible at your practice sessions. As a general rule, aim for one ball between three.

- **PLAYERS:** Many of the drills in this book use three players at each station. This will provide each player with many opportunities to practice the particular skill for which the drill is being used. As a general guide the maximum number at any station should not be more than five, as lack of participation will lead only to boredom and consequently ineffective practice. If the drill is being used as part of a fitness programme, four players at each station will give a desired work/rest ratio of 3:1.

4. INTRODUCING DRILLS

- Set up everything you need for the drill; cones, footballs, goals, etc.

- Give the drill a suitable name.

- Explain the aim of the drill.

- Begin slowly. Walk players through a new drill so that it is understood by all.

- Use a small group of players to perform the drill at the desired pace.

5. INCREASING THE DIFFICULTY OF DRILLS

DRILLS CAN BE MADE MORE DEMANDING BY:

- Adding more footballs

- Adding defenders

- Adding more stations

- Emphasising speed

- Decreasing the number of players

6. COACHES' RESPONSIBILITY

- As coaches, we have a tremendous responsibility both to the game of Gaelic Football and to our players. It is imperative that we help players to develop all the skills of the game to their full and unique potential, thus ensuring that Gaelic Football is always played to the highest standard possible, bringing maximum enjoyment and satisfaction to players and spectators alike. It would be most gratifying if this publication should help you as a coach to carry out that responsibility in an effective manner.

Legend

★ ....Player

● ....Football

★● ....Player with a football

◉ ....Defender

→ ....Player Movement

--→ ....Ball Movement

→--→ ....Player & Ball Movement

A ....Station or Cone

COACH ....Coach

〜〜〜〜→ ....Rolling Ball

10m or |—15m—| ....Distance

Note: Where distance is not stated or given
between cones, assume 20m as the norm.

HP --→ K --→ SR --→ ....Ball Movement Abbreviations

HP	=	Handpass	HK	=	Hook Kick
SR	=	Solo Run	PU	=	Pick Up
K	=	Kick	BD	=	Blockdown
PK	=	Punt Kick	C	=	Catch

Legend (cont.)

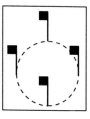

Circle Drill

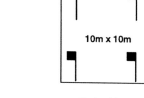

10m x 10m

Grid Size

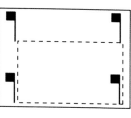

Rectangle Drill

Line Drill

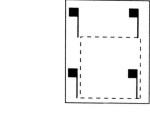

Square Drill

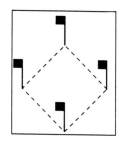

Diamond Drill

Triangle
Drill

Example of a Typical Drill

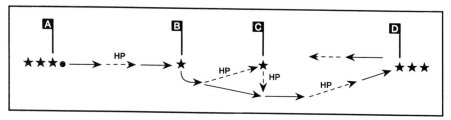

1. Three players at A and D. One player at B and C. One football at A.

2. A pass to B. Join B.

3. B turns, passes to C, receives return and passes to D. Join D.

4. D pass to C. Join C.

5. C turns, passes to B, receives return and passes to A. Join A.

6. Drill continues.

~ KICKING DRILLS ~

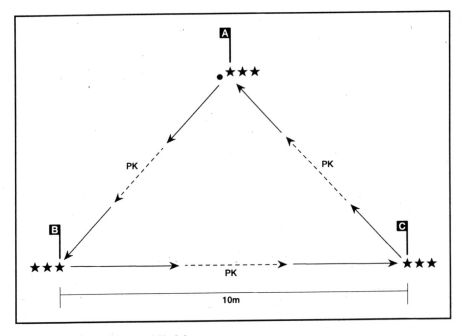

1. Repetitive Short Kicking:

1. Three or more players at A, B and C. One or more footballs at A.

2. A kicks to B and joins B.

3. B kicks to C and joins C.

4. C kicks to A and joins A.

5. Drill continues.

6. Reverse direction. Increase distance.

7. **Variation:** Introduce one defender who attempts to intercept. Kickers must choose receiver and follow their kick.

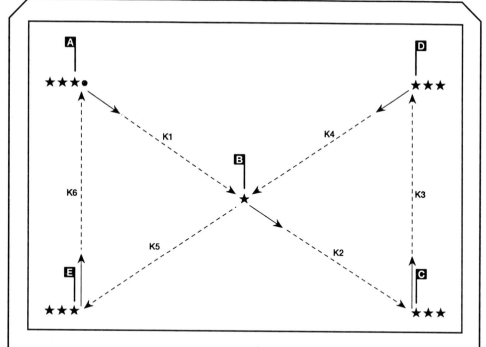

2. Figure Eight Kicking:

1. One player at station B, three or more players at A, E, C and D. One or more footballs at A.

2. Beginning at A, the ball is kicked in a figure 8 pattern as shown. (A to B, B to C, C to D, D to B, B to E, E to A.)

3. Players follow their kick and replace at the next station.

4. Drill continues.

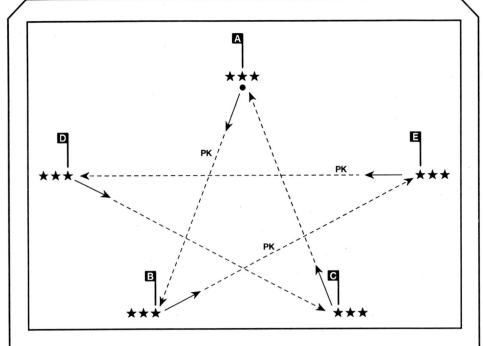

3. Starkick:

1. Three or more players at each station 20/30m apart. One or more footballs at A.

2. Golden Rule: Kick and follow.

3. A kick to B, join B. B kick to C, join C. C kick to D, join D. D kick to E, join E. E kick to A, join A.

4. Drill continues.

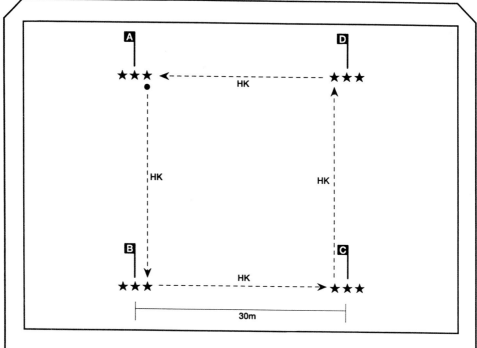

4. Kicking in Squares:

1.   Three or more players at A, B, C and D. One or more footballs at A.

2.   A kicks to B, B to C, C to D, D to A.

3.   Drill continues

4.   **Variations:**

   1) Players follow their kick.

   2) Players remain at their station.

   3) Reverse direction.

   4) Players work in pairs, putting token pressure on all kicks.

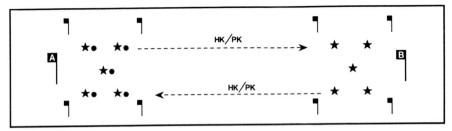

5. Box it Drill:

1. Five or more players in Grid A and Grid B, 20 - 40 m. apart. Two to five footballs in grid A.

2. Players kick from A to B, who will return. Remain in your own grid.

3. Scoring: Any kick from Grid A which successfully falls (or is caught) inside Grid B equals 1 point. First to reach specified total, e.g. 10, is declared the winner.

4. Vary the distance between the grids.

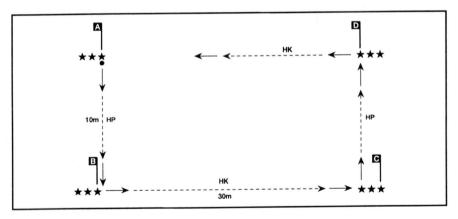

6. Hook and Pass:

1. Three or more players at A, B, C and D. One or more footballs at A.

2. A handpasses to B, B kicks to C, C handpasses to D, who kicks to A.

3. Players follow their pass/kick to the next station.

4. Drill continues.

5. Reverse direction.

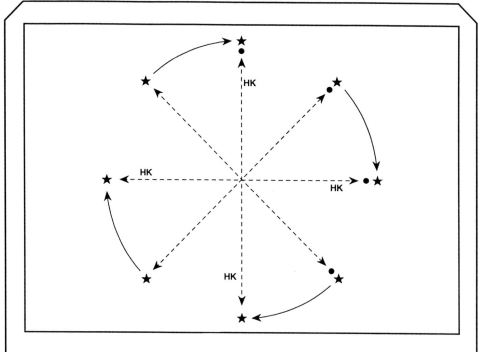

7. Circle Kicking:

1. Players work in pairs. One football per pair.

2. Kick across the circle to partner.

3. All players are moving in a clockwise direction.

4. Drill continues.

5. Reverse direction. Vary distance between players.

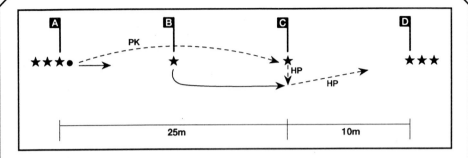

8. Kick and Handpass:

1. Three or more players at A and D. One player at B and C. One football at A.
2. A kicks to C and runs to station B.
3. B runs to C, receives from C and handpasses to D. Join D.
4. D kicks to B and runs to station C.
5. C runs to B, receives from B and handpasses to A. Join A.
6. Drill continues.
7. **Variation:** Introduce defender between B and C. B must change direction to receive pass.

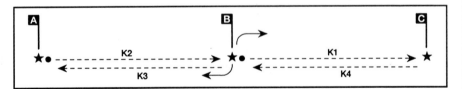

9. Return, Turn Drill:

1. One player at A, B and C. One football at A and B. Stations 15-20m. apart.
2. B kicks to C, turns quickly and receives kick from A.
3. B returns to A, turns quickly and receives from B.
4. Drill continues.
5. Rotate middle man. Limit time or number of kicks.

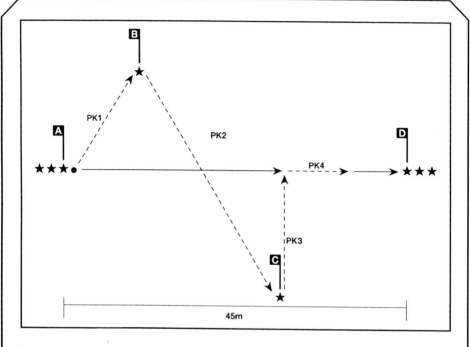

10. Kick and Support:

1. Three players or more at A and D. One stationary player at B and C. One football at A.

2. A kicks to B and runs in the direction of D.

3. B kicks to to C and C returns to A, who then kicks to D.

4. D kicks to C and runs in the direction of A.

5. C kicks to B and B returns to D, who then kicks to A.

6. Drill continues.

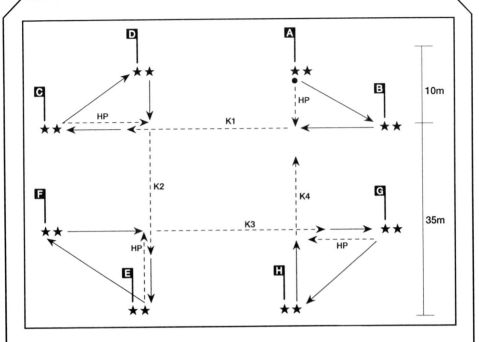

11. Pass, Kick, Pass Drill:

1.   Eight stations, two or more players at each station. One or more footballs at A.

2.   A handpass to B, running on. B kick to C and join C. A join B.

3.   C handpass to D running on. D kick to E and join E. C join D.

4.   E handpass to F, running on. F kick to G and join G. E join F.

5.   G handpass to H, running on. H kick to A and join A. G join H.

6.   Drill continues as before.

7.   Golden Rule: Follow your kick or pass to the back of the next station.

8.   **Variation:** Introduce defender to pressurise all hand passes.

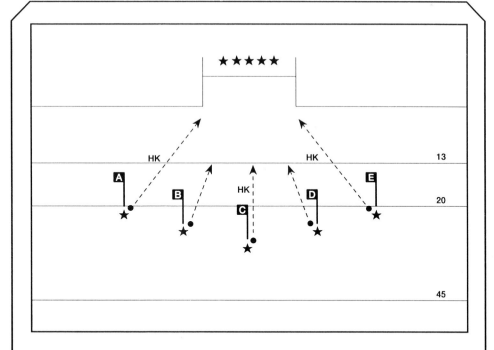

12. Target Kick:

1. Players work in pairs. One player at each station, with partner behind the goal. One football per pair.

2. One or more attempt at each station. Record score.

3. When completed change roles with partner.

4. Drill continues.

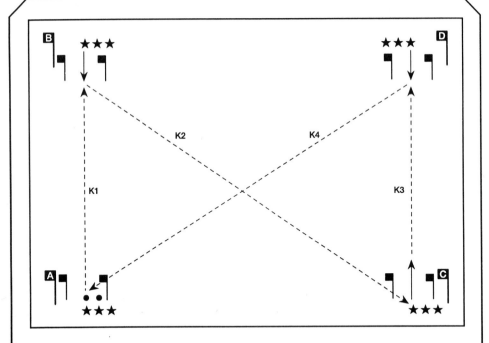

13. Four Corner Kick and Catch:

1. Four stations, 30-40m. apart. Three or more players at each station. Two or more footballs at A.

2. A kicks between the cones at B. B catches and kicks between the cones at C. C catches and kicks between the cones at D. D catches and kicks between the cones at A.

3. Players remain at their station and catches must be made between the cones.

4. Drill continues.

5. **Variation:** Players follow their kick.

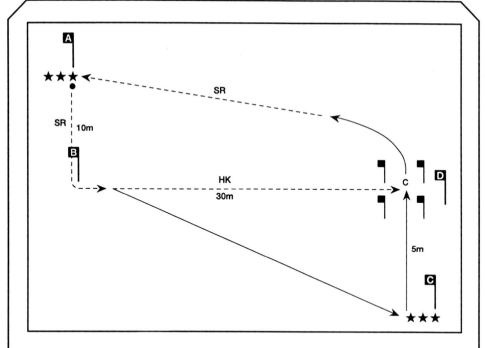

14. Hook and Catch Drill:

1. Three stations, one grid, D. Three or more players at A and C. Two or more footballs at A.

2. A soloes around station B, kicks into Grid D. Join C.

3. Player at C, with a timed run, catches the ball in the grid and soloes back to station A.

4. Drill continues.

5. **Variation:** Introduce defender at A. Token pressure on solo run to B and then attempt to block down kick at B.

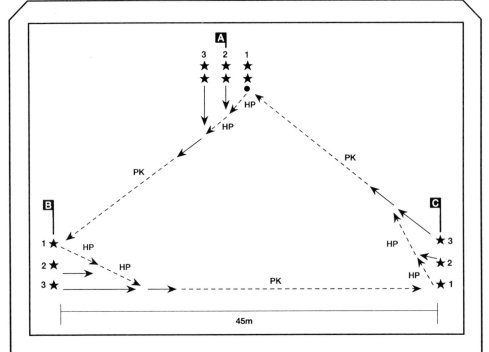

15. Pass, Pass and Kick Drill:

1. Three stations, six players at A, three at B and C. One football at A.
2. Player 1 at A handpass to 2 moving forward, who handpasses to player 3.
3. Player 3 kicks to B who repeats the pass, pass kick sequence to C.
4. Groups follow their kick to the next station. Alternate positions.
5. Drill continues.
6. **Variation:** Introduce defender between stations.

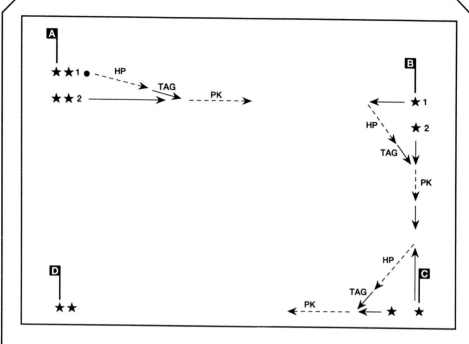

16. Handpass, Tag and Kick:

1. Four or more stations. Four players at A, two at the other stations. One football at A.

2. Player 1 at A handpass ahead to player 2, and run to tag him.

3. Player 2 kicks to B, where player 1 catches, handpasses to player 2 and runs to tag him.

4. Player 2 kicks to C and the drill continues in this manner.

5. Players move in pairs, following the kick to the next station.

6. After the handpass is made the player must run in support to touch/tag his partner.

7. **Variation:** Add a defender at each station. Intercept either the kick or the pass. Both players get free to receive and they support each other. Tagging continues.

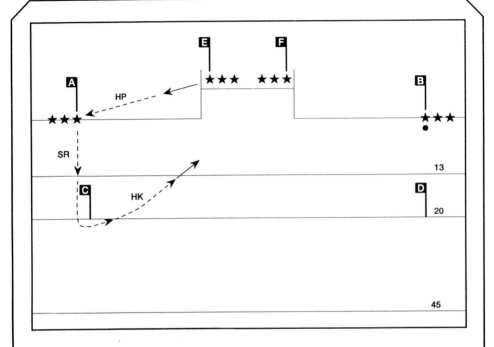

17. Solo and Hook Drill:

1. Three players or more at A, B, E and F. Cones at C and D. One or more footballs at A and B.

2. A soloes around C and shoots. Join E.

3. E retrieves ball and passes to A. Join A.

4. Drill continues on both sides.

5. **Variation:** A follows his kick and joins F, B follows his kick and joins E. Drill continues in this manner.

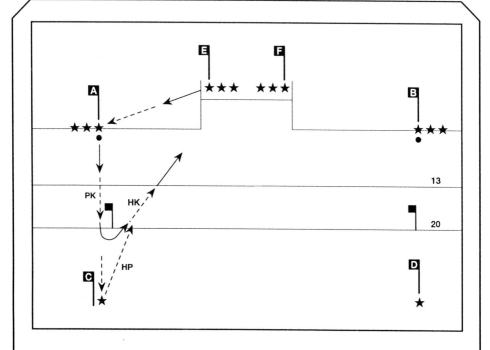

18. Pass and Return:

1. Three players or more at A. and E. One or more footballs at A. One stationary player at C.

2. A kicks to C, follows, receives return from C, and shoots. Join E.

3. E retrieves and passes to A. Join A.

4. Drill continues on both sides.

5. **Variation:**

   1) Place three or more players at C. C pass to A and join E. A join C.

   2) Introduce defender at A.

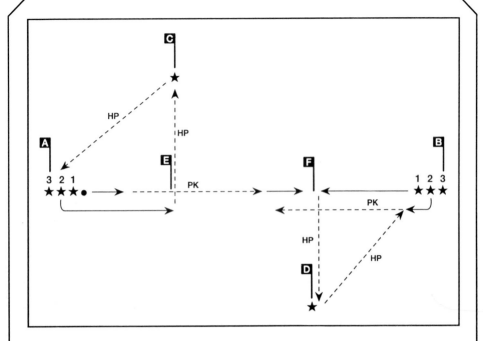

19. Pass and Support:

1. Three or more players at A and B. One stationary player at C and D. Cones at E and F. One football at A.

2. A1 kicks to B1, who receives at F. Join B.

3. B1 handpasses to D. Join A.

4. D handpasses to B2 who kicks to A. Join A.

5. A2 receives at E and handpasses to C. Join B.

6. C handpasses to A3 who kicks to and joins B.

7. Drill continues.

8. **Variation.:**

   a) Switch Station D to the opposite side in line with cone F.

   b) One player at C, is always running between Station C and D in support of A & B.

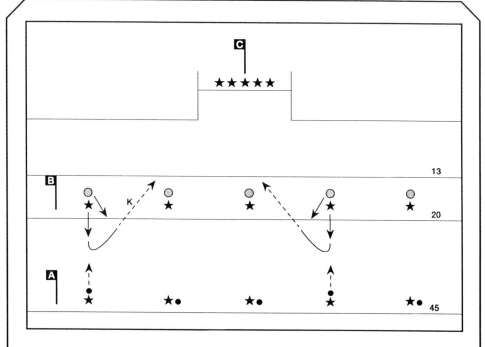

20. Pressure Shooting Drill:

1.   Two players , one defending, one attacking at Station B. One player, with one or more footballs, at A. Five players retrieving at C.

2.   A kicks to attacking player at B, who shoots for a score, under token pressure initially.

3.   C returns ball to A.

4.   Defending player applies full pressure.

5.   Rotate players after a specified time.

6.   Drill continues.

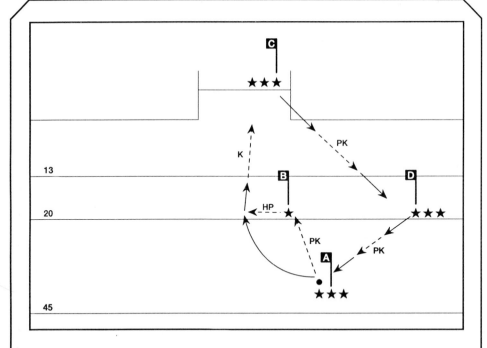

21. Kick and Score:

1. Three or more players at A, C and D. One stationary player at B. One or more footballs at A.

2. A kicks to B, takes return and shoots. A join C.

3. C retrieves and kicks to D. Join D.

4. D kicks to A. Join A.

5. Drill continues.

6. **Variation:**

   1) Place two players at B. A kick to B. Player B turns and shoots. A join B.

   2) Use the same drill on the left side of the pitch.

~ HANDPASS DRILLS ~

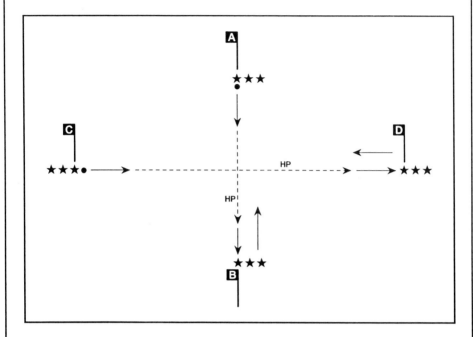

1. Criss Cross:

1. Three or more players at A, B, C and D. One football at A and C.

2. A pass to B. Join B.   C pass to D. Join D.

3. B pass to A. Join A. D pass to C. Join C.

4. Drill continues

5. **Variation:** Add more stations.

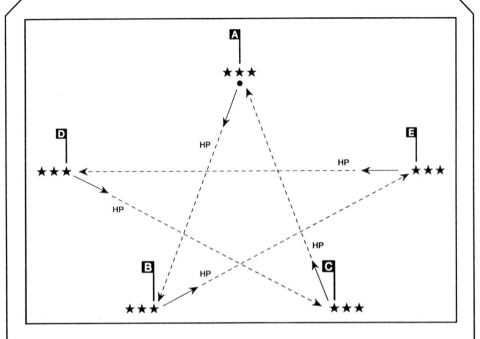

2. Starpass:

1. Three or more players at A, B, C, D and E. One or more footballs at A.

2. Golden Rule: Follow your pass.

3. A pass to B, B to E, E to D, D to C, C to A.

4. Drill continues.

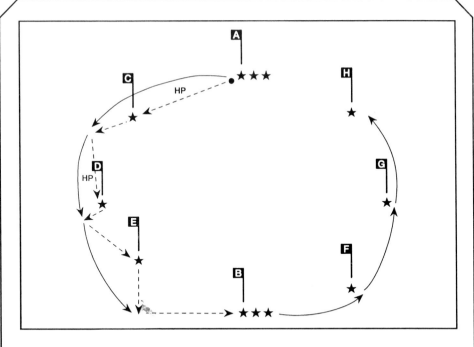

3. Pass and Return Circle Drill:

1. Three or more players at A and B. One stationary player at C, D, E, F and G. One or more footballs at A and B.

2. A pass to C, run, take return, pass to D, take return, pass to E, take return, pass to B. Join B.

3. B repeats with F, G and H.

4. Drill continues

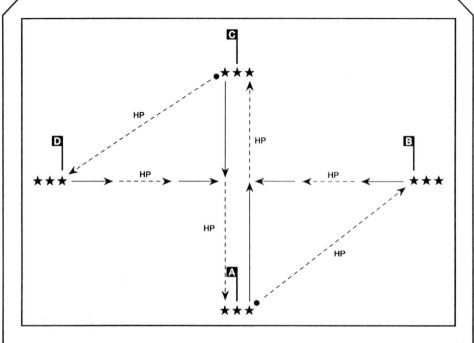

4. Cross Drill:

1. Three or more players at A, B, C and D. One football at A and C.

2. A and C begin together. A pass to B, run on, recieve return from B, pass to C. Join C.

3. C pass to D, run on, take return, pass to A. Join A.

4. B and D follow their pass to the opposite line.

5. Drill continues.

6. **Variation:** Use stationary player at B and D.

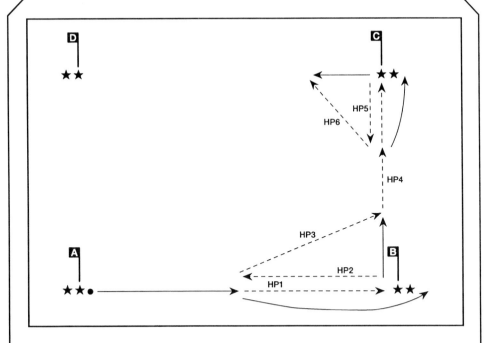

5. Give and Go:

1. Two or more players at A, B, C and D. One football at A.

2. A pass to B. Run on and receive return pass from B. B now breaks towards C. A pass to B and join B.

3. B pass to C, takes return from C. C breaks towards D. B pass to C and join C.

4. Drill continues.

5. **Variation:** Introduce defender between A and B, B and C etc. who exerts full pressure to prevent the passes.

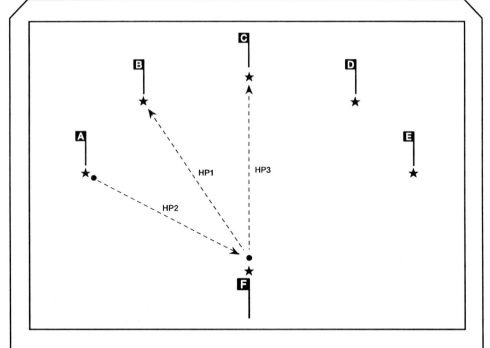

6. Quickness Drill:

1.   Arrange five or more players in a semi-circle, A to E, facing player at F. One football at A and F.

2.   F pass to B. Receive from A, pass to C, receive from B etc.

3.   E replace F. F join A, who moves to B.

4.   Drill continues.

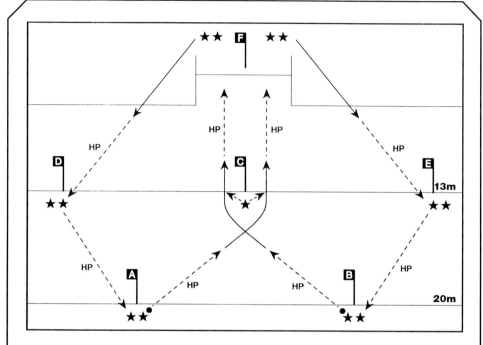

7. Pass and Score:

1. Two or more players at A, B, D and E. One stationery player at C, and four players at F. One or more footballs at A and B.

2. A handpass to C, take return and fistpass over the bar to score. Join F.

3. B handpass to C, take return and fistpass over the bar to score. Join F.

4. Players at F recover ball, pass to E and D and join E and D.

5. E and D pass to B and A, and join B and A respectively.

6. Next players at A and B repeat.

7. Drill continues.

8. **Variation:**

    1) Use one ball only, at A. A pass to C. A and B run towards C as before. C decides to pass to either A or B. Receiver scores. Join F.

    2) Introduce defender at C.

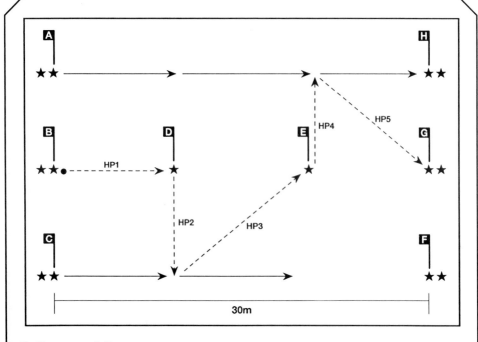

8. Pass and Support:

1. Two or more players at A, B, C and F, G, H. One stationary player at D and E. One football at B.

2. B pass to D. A, B and C move together towards D. D pass to A or C.

3. C receives from D, pass to E. E pass to A or C.

4. A receives from E, pass to G. A, B and C join F, G and H.

5. G pass to E and drill continues.

6. **Variation:** Introduce defender at D and E.

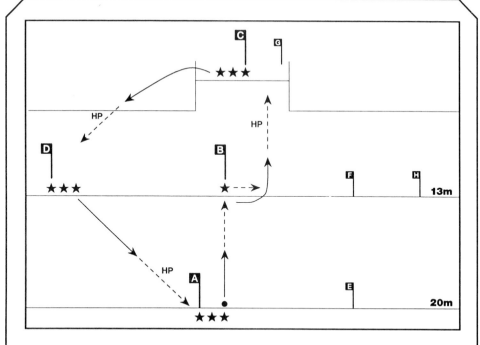

9. Pass, Receive and Score:

1. Three players at A, C and D. One player at B. One or more footballs at A.

2. A pass to B, take return and handpass over the bar for a score. A join C.

3. C pass to D and join D.

4. D pass to A and join A.

5. Drill continues.

6. **Variation:**

    1) Player at B turns and scores. A replace B.

    2) Introduce players at E, F, G and H.

    3) Introduce defender at B.

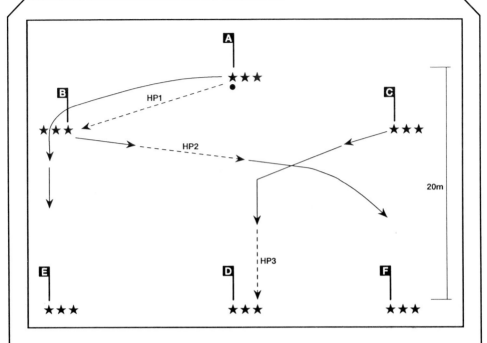

10. Pass and Go Behind:

1. Two or more players at A, B, C, D, E and F. One football at A.

2. A pass to B. Go behind B and run to E. Join E.

3. B pass to C running in towards line A. Go behind C and run to F. Join F.

4. C pass to D and join D.

5. D pass to F, F to E and E to A on return.

6. Drill continues.

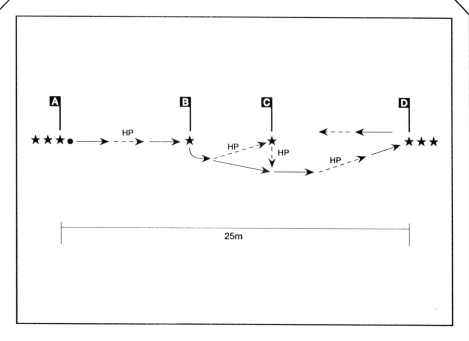

11. Pass, Turn and Go Drill:

1. Three players at A and D. One player at B and C. One football at A.

2. A pass to B. Join B.

3. B turns, passes to C, receives return and passes to D.Join D.

4. D pass to C. Join C.

5. C turns, passes to B, receives return and passes to A. Join A.

6. Drill continues.

7. **Variation:** Introduce defenders at B and C.

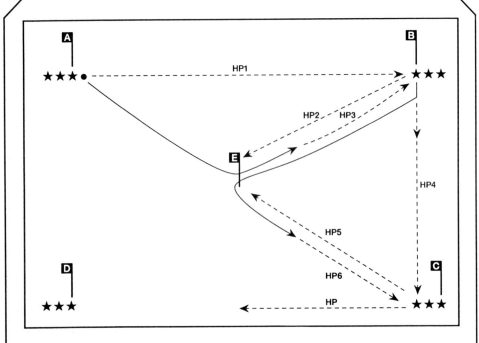

12. Pass, Receive, Return Drill:

1. Three players or more at A, B, C and D. One or more footballs at A. Centre cone at E.

2. A pass to B. Run to centre cone E. Receive pass from B and return to B. Join B.

3. B pass to C. Run to centre cone E. Receive from C, return to C. Join C.

4. Repeat at C and D.

5. Drill continues.

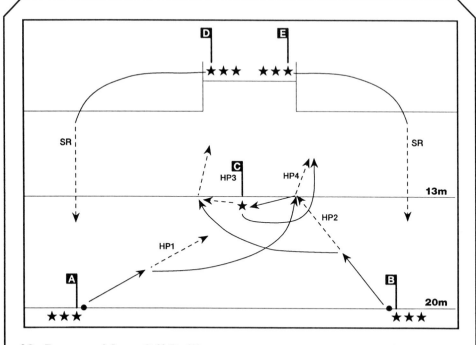

13. Pass and Lay Off Drill:

1. Three or more players at A, B, D and E. One player at C. One or more footballs at A and B.

2. A pass to C. Run and receive from B on the 13m line.

3. B breaks past and receives from C. B fist pass over the bar. Join D.

4. C now turns, receives from A and fistpasses over the bar. Join E.

5. A replace C.

6. D and E solo and pass to A and B. Join A and B.

7. Drill continues.

~ CATCHING DRILLS ~

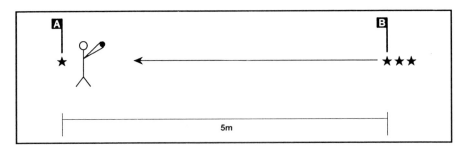

1. Jump and Catch:

1. Coach or player holds football at shoulder/head height at A.

2. Three players or more at B.

3. B runs, jumps, catches ball, and takes from coach's hand.

4. Return ball to coach. Rejoin B.

5. Drill continues.

6. **Variation:** As player approaches, the coach throws the ball upwards.

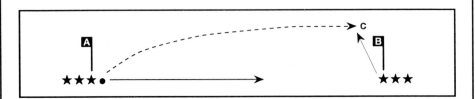

2. Run to Catch:

1. Three players or more at A and B, 5-10 metres apart. One football at A.

2. A throws or punches ball to B, who catches overhead. A join B.

3. Repeat from B.

4. Drill continues.

5. **Variation:** Increase distance. Use kickpass.

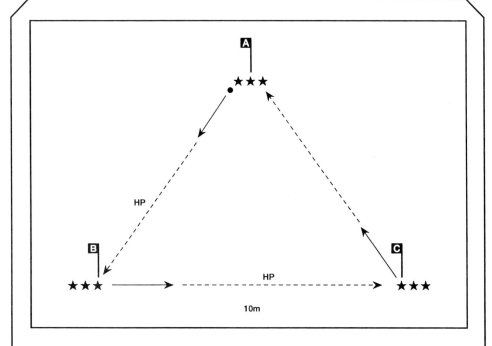

3. Catch and Move:

1. Three or more players at A, B and C. One or more footballs at A.

2. A throw/punch to B. Join B.

3. B catches overhead, punches to C. Join C.

4. C catches, punches to A. Join A.

5. Drill continues.

6. **Variation:** Introduce defensive player in the middle.

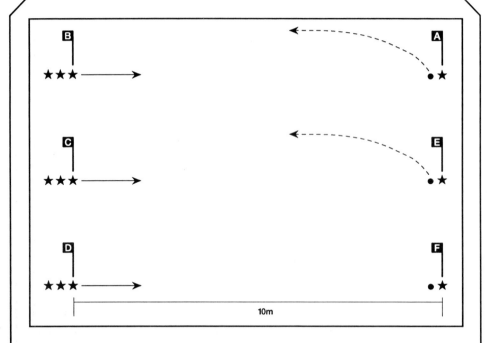

4. Run, Catch and Return:

1. Three or more players at B, C and D. One player at A, E and F, with a football each.

2. A throw/punch to B. B runs, jumps, catches overhead, passes back to A. Rejoin line B.

3. A continues to serve until last player in line, who replaces him.

4. Drill continues.

5. **Variation:**

   1. Players work in pairs at B, C and D.

   2. Increase distance. Use kick.

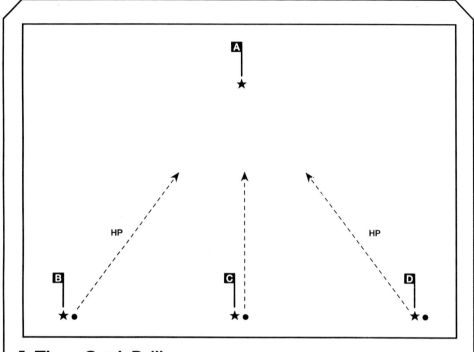

5. Three Catch Drill:

1. One player at A, B, C and D, 5-10 metres apart. One football at B, C and D.

2. B throw/punch high to A, who catches and returns.

3. C throw/punch low to A, who catches and returns.

4. D throw/punch at chest height. A catches and returns.

5. Rotate after specified number of catches.

6. Drill continues.

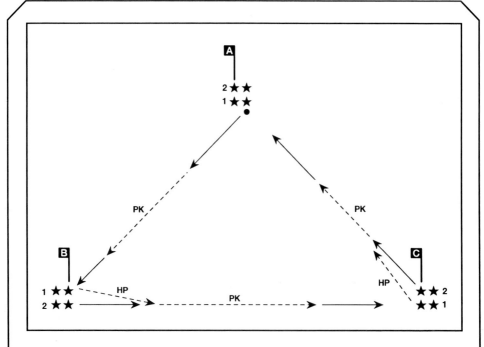

6. Catch and Pass:

1. Four or more players at A, B and C, 30m apart, working in pairs on chest and low catches. One or more footballs at A.

2. A1 kicks to B. A1 and A2 join B.

3. B1 catches, passes to B2, who kicks to C. B1 and B2 join C.

4. C1 catches, passes to C2, who kicks to A. C1 and C2 join A.

5. Drill continues, with players changing roles.

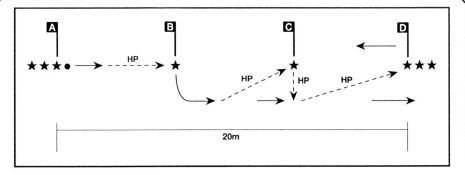

7. Pass, Catch, Pass Drill:

1. Three or more players at A and D. One player at C and D. One football at A.
2. A pass to B. Join B.
3. B turn and pass to C, take return from C and pass to D. Join D.
4. D pass to C. Join C.
5. C turn, pass to B, take return, pass to A. Join A.
6. Drill continues.
7. **Variation:** Introduce defender at B and C.

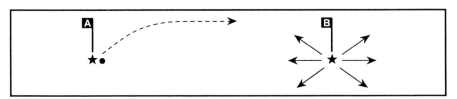

8. Move to Catch:

1. One player at A and B, 10 metres apart. One football at A.
2. A throw/punch to B, varying the direction of the punch - to the side, behind, in front.
3. A adjust position to catch overhead.
4. Change roles after specified time.
5. Drill continues.
6. **Variation:** Introduce defender at B.

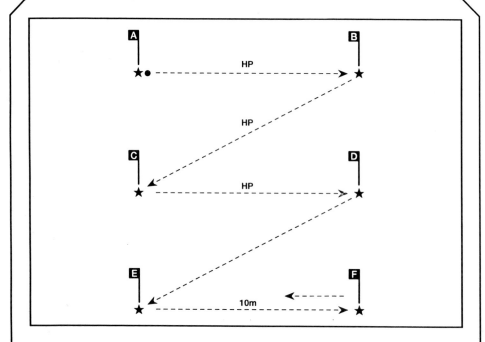

9. Crossball Drill:

1. One player at A, B, C, D, E and F. One football at A.

2. A pass to B, B to C, C to D, etc as shown.

3. When F receives, reverse movement of the ball to E.

4. Drill continues.

5. **Variation:**

   1) Add one or more defender who tries to intercept passes.

   2) All players follow their pass.

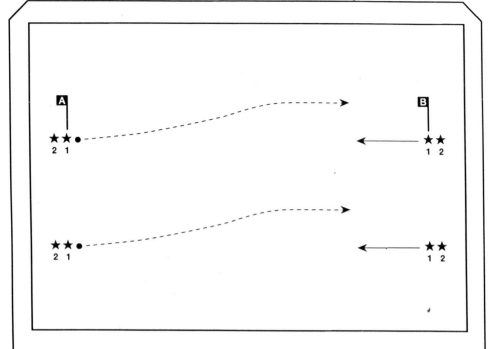

10. Catch under Pressure:

1. Four or more players in pairs at A and B, 10m apart. One football at A.

2. A throw/punch to B. B2 attempts to catch, with interference from B1, in front.

3. B2 throw/punch to A. A2 attempts to catch, with interference from A1.

4. Drill continues.

5. **Variation:**

   1) Repeat drill with player 1 attempting to catch in front as player 2 interferes from behind.

   2) Increase distance and use kick.

   3) Both players contest the catch.

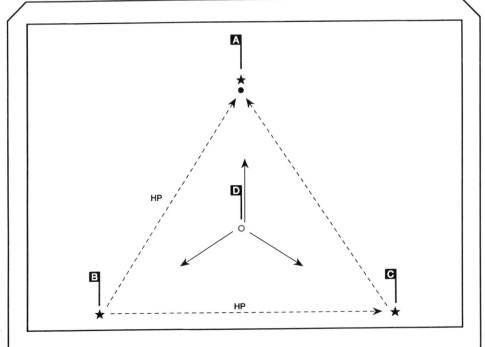

11. Work the Middle Man:

1. One player at A, B, C and D, 5-10m apart, with one football at A.

2. A, B and C throw/punch to each other and attempt to catch on the body.

3. D offers token opposition as players attempt to catch.

4. Replace D after specified time.

5. Drill continues.

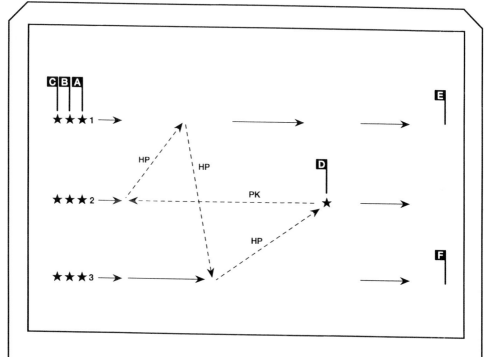

12. Catch and Support Drill:

1. Nine or more players at A, B and C, working in threes. Stationary player at D with a football. Cones at E and F.

2. D kicks to line A.

3. A2 passes to A1 or A3, who run in support. (A1 in diagram). A1 pass to A3.

4. A3 pass to D. All three players join E and F.

5. Drill continues with the next line B.

6. Repeat from E, F.

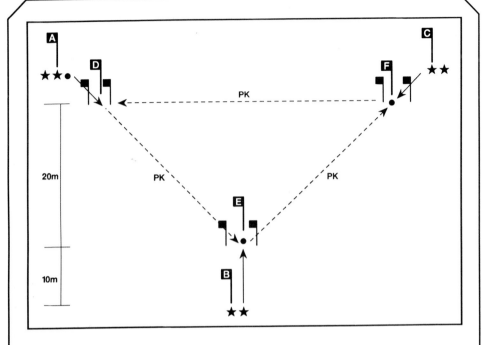

13. Kick and Catch:

1. Three or more players at A, B and C. One football at A. Cones at D,E,F.

2. A kicks to B, who breaks to receive and catch between cones at E. A joins B.

3. B kicks to C, who receives at F. B join C.

4. C kick to A, who receives at D. C join A.

5. Drill continues.

6. **Variation:** Introduce defender at A, B and C.

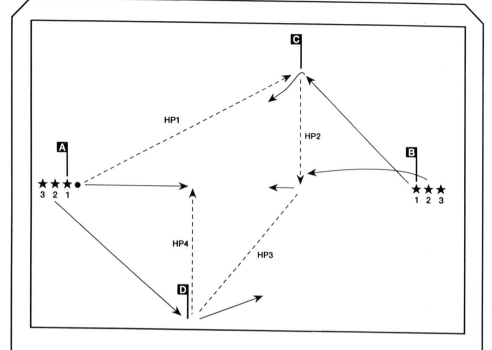

14. Handpass and Catch:

1. Three or more players at A and B, 10-20m apart. One football at A. Cones at C and D.

2. A1 handpass to B1, who breaks to receive and catch at C. A1 join B.

3. B2 breaks in the direction of A to recieve from B1. B1 join A.

4. B2 pass to A2, who breaks to recieve and catch at D. B2 join A.

5. A2 pass to A3, running in the direction of B. A2 join B.

6. Drill continues.

~ SOLO RUN DRILLS ~

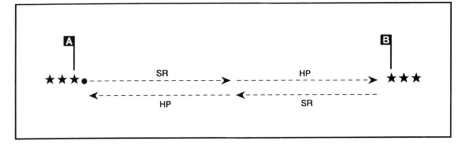

1. Solo and Handpass:

1. Three players or more at A and B. One football at A.

2. A solo and handpass to B. Join B.

3. B repeats. Join A.

4. Drill continues.

5. **Variation:** Increase distance and use kickpass.

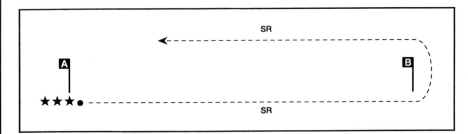

2. Out and Back:

1. Three players or more at A. One or more footballs at A. Cone at B.

2. A solo around B and back to A.

3. Handpass to next player.

4. Drill continues.

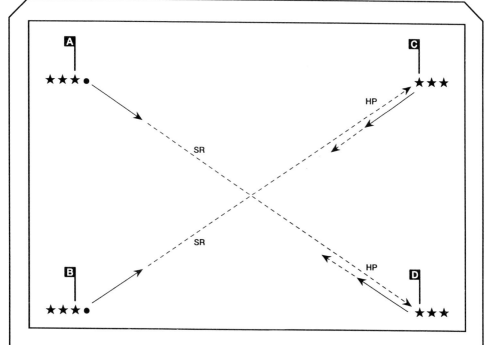

3. Crossroads:

1. Three or more players at A, B, C and D. One or more footballs at A & B.

2. A solo to D, B solo to C simultaneously.

3. A handpass to D, B to C.

4. D solo and pass to A, and C to B.

5. Drill continues.

6. **Variation:** Add more stations.

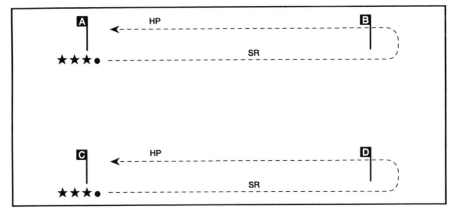

4. Relay Run:

1. Three or more players at A and C. One football at A and C. Cones at B and D.

2. Players solo in relays around B and D and handpass to next player.

3. First group to complete the course are declared winners.

4. Vary distance, number of teams, number of cones etc.

5. Drill continues.

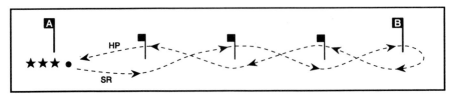

5. In and Out Drill:

1. Three or more players at A. One or more footballs at A. Arrange 3-5 cones between A and B.

2. A solo around cones, using both feet.

3. Handpass to next player at A.

4. Drill continues.

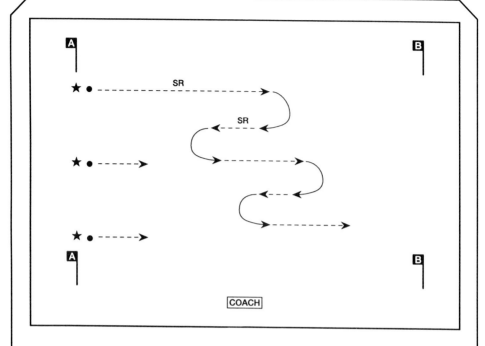

6. On the Whistle Drill:

1. Three or more players at A, each with a football.

2. A solo towards B.

3. Coach blows whistle. Players change direction and soloing foot.

4. Drill continues with players changing feet and direction on coach's whistle.

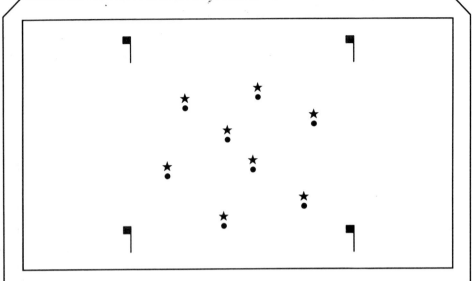

7. Last Man In:

1. Any number of players within the grid with a football each.

2. Players solo and move about the grid freely.

3. Players attempt to legally disposses each other as they move.

4. Player leaves the grid when his/her ball touches the ground.

5. Last remaining player in possesion is declared the winner.

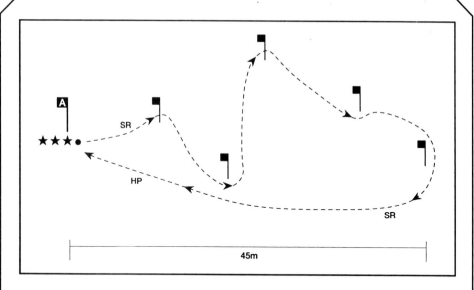

8. Speed Solo:

1. Three players or more at A. One or more footballs. Arrange cones at random.

2. Solo around cones and back at speed.

3. Drill continues.

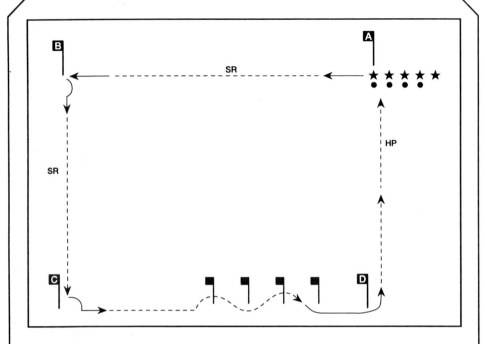

9. Combined Solo:

1. Eight or more players at A. Three or more footballs at A. Cones at B, C and D.

2. a) Player 1 solo at speed to B. Dummy solo at B. Player 2 begins.

   b) Solo with opposite foot from B to C. Sidestep at C. Player 3 begins.

   c) Solo zig zag between cones to D. Player 4 begins.

   d) Solo around D and back to A. Handpass to next player.

3. Drill continues.

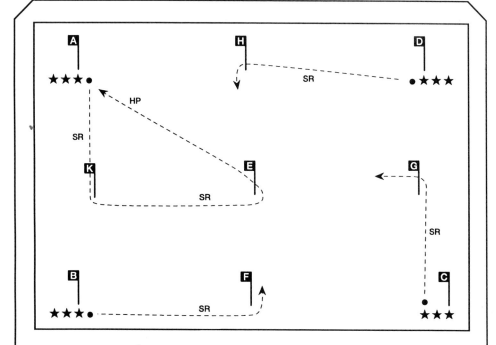

10. Centre Cone Drill:

1. Three players or more at A, B, C and D. One football at A, B, C and D. Cones at E, F, G, H and K.

2. Players solo in an anticlockwise direction to the next cone: A to K, B to F, C to G, D to H.

3. Each player then soloes around centre cone E and back to original starting point. Pass to next player.

4. Drill continues.

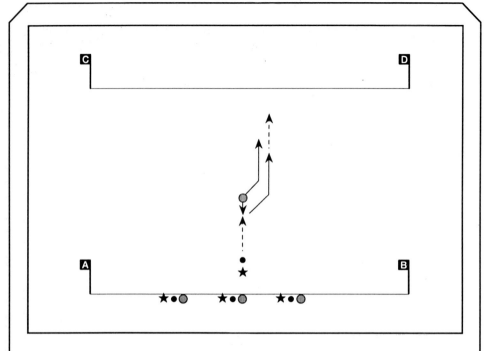

11. One on One:

1. Six players or more working in pairs, one attacker with a football, one defender.

2. Attacker soloes across the grid from AB to CD. The defender, applying full pressure, attempts to dispossess. Remain at CD.

3. Next pair at AB begin.

4. Reverse roles on return.

5. Drill continues.

~ INDIVIDUAL DEFENSIVE DRILLS ~

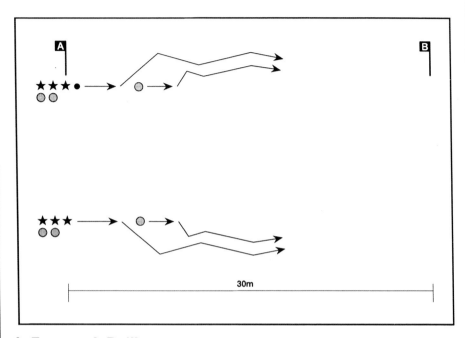

I. Footwork Drill:

1.   Six players or more at A, working in pairs. No football required.

2.   Attacker moves forward towards B in a zig zag manner.

3.   Defender reacts and retreats, staying between the attacker and station B.

4.   Both players remain at B.

5.   Drill continues from A.

6.   Reverse roles.

7.   **Variation:** Add a football at A.

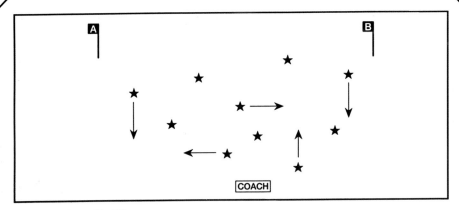

2. Reaction Drill:

1. Any number of players, facing the coach, between A and B.

2. Coach instructs and players respond to calls: eg left, right, back, forward etc.

3. Drill continues for a specified time.

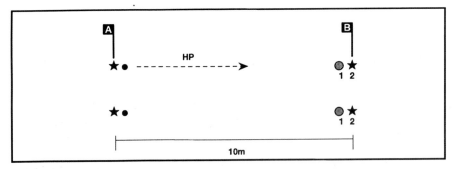

3. Flick It Up:

1. Any number of players working in threes, one player at A, two players at B, one of whom acts as a defender. One football at A.

2. A punch the ball to B2 who catches overhead. As he brings the ball under control, B1 attempts to flick the ball from B2 with the open hand.

3. A join B1, B1 join B2, and B2 join A.

4. Drill continues.

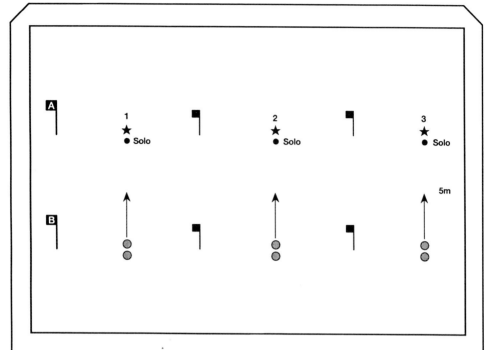

4. Flick it Away:

1. Any number of players, working in threes. One player at A, each with a football. Two players at B.

2. Players at A solo the ball in a stationary position; player 1 faces his opponent, player 2 is side on to his opponent, player 3 has his back to his opponent.

3. Players at B control their run to A to dispossess by flicking the ball away.

4. B recover ball and replace A. A join B.

5. Drill continues.

6. **Variation:** Place players, currently at B, behind cone at A. Players with the ball continue to solo as before, with defenders now moving in from A to dispossess.

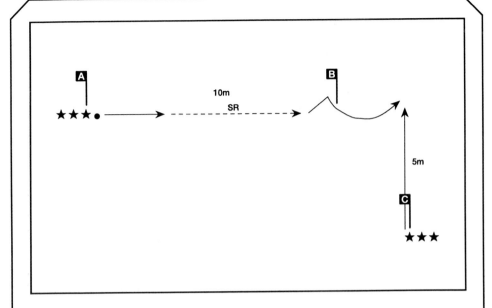

5. Solo and Flick:

1. Three or more players at A and C. Cone at B. Two or more footballs at A.

2. A solo to B, sidestep at B, stop and look ahead, hold ball in a natural position.

3. C times his run to flick the ball from A.

4. A join C. C join A.

5. Drill continues.

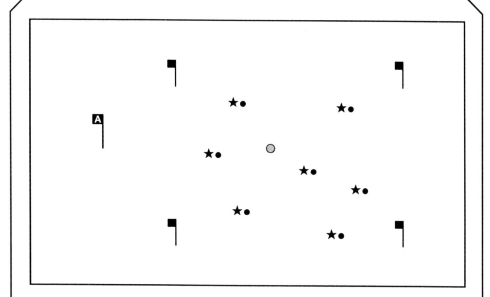

6. Against the Clock:

1. Any number of players in Grid A, with a football each. One defender only in the grid.

2. Defender attempts to dispossess as players move about the grid.

3. The defender who dispossesses all players in the shortest time is delcared the winner.

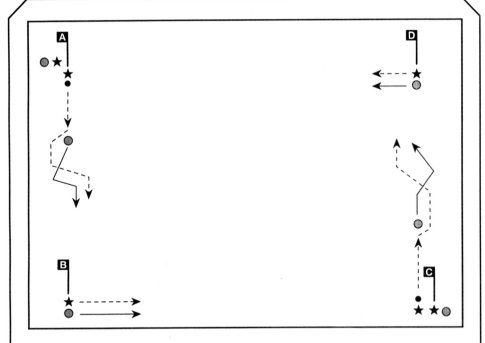

7. One on One:

1. Four players at A and C, two players at B and D. One football at A and C.

2. Players work in pairs, one defending, one attacking.

3. Attacker at A moves forward towards B, using solo, sidestep etc, while defender tries to dispossess. Both join B.

4. Pair at C begin at the same time as A.

5. Players at B, receiving from A and players at D, receiving from C, move to C and A respectively.

6. Drill continues.

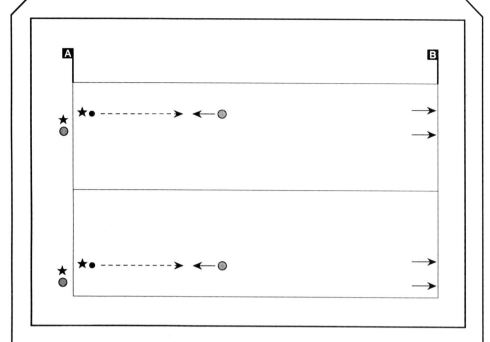

8. Hands and Feet Drill:

1. Six or more players, working in pairs, at A. Cone at B, 20m away. One football or more at A.

2. A attacks to reach B; defender works hard to dispossess, staying between player A and cone B.

3. **Variation**s:

   A) Defender chases from behind.

   B) Defender comes at the player side on.

4. Players join B.

5. Next pair go.

6. Drill continues. Repeat from B.

7. **Variation:** One player at B who kickpasses to the attacker, who gets free to receive.

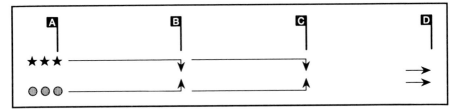

9. Shoulder to Shoulder:

1.　Any number of players in pairs at A. Cones at B, C and D.

2.　A run towards D; players shoulder each other at B and C. Join D.

3.　Drill continues.

4.　Repeat from D.

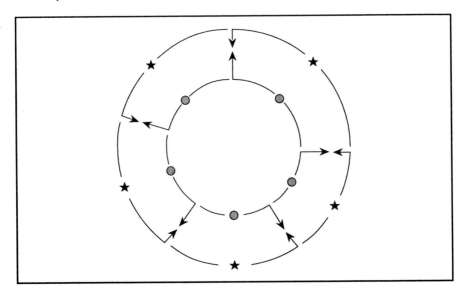

10. Circle Shoulder Drill:

1.　Any number of players, working in pairs aranged in a circle formation.

2.　Players move in the same direction, regularly shouldering each other.

3.　Reverse direction.

4.　Drill continues for a specified time.

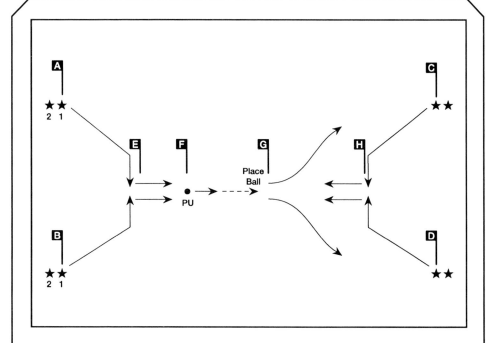

11. Run and Shoulder:

1. Two or more players at A, B, C and D. Cones at E, F, G and H. One football at F. All cones 10m apart.

2. Player 1 at A and B run and shoulder at cone E. Both players continue towards cone F where leading player picks up the ball. Replace ball at Cone G. A join C and B join D.

3. Player 1 at C and D repeat from this end. After ball is picked, replace at F.

4. Drill continues.

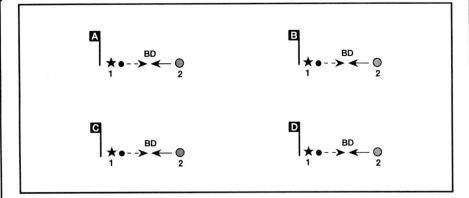

12. Blockdown Drill:

1.   Arrange players in pairs at A, B, C and D. One football between each pair.

2.   Player 1 in a stationery position, kicks, player 2 attempts blockdown.

3.   Reverse roles after specified time.

4.   Drill continues.

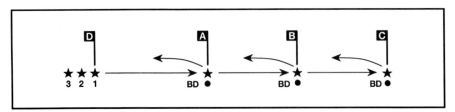

13. Kick, Block and Move:

1.   One player, with a football, at A, B and C, 5m apart.

2.   Three or more players at D.

3.   Players at D move in turn to block down at A, B and C.

4.   D1 block at A. A join D. D1 block at B. B join A. D1 block at C. C join B. D1 join C.

5.   Drill continues with D2.

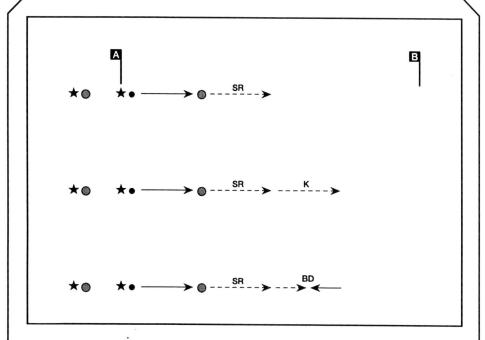

14. Solo and Block:

1. Two stations, A and B, 30m apart. Any number of players, working in pairs, at A. Two or more footballs at A.

2. Attacker moves towards B, soloes twice and then must kick.

3. Defender attempts blockdown.

4. Join B. Reverse roles on return.

5. Drill continues

6. **Variation:** Defender attempts the blockdown from behind and from the side.

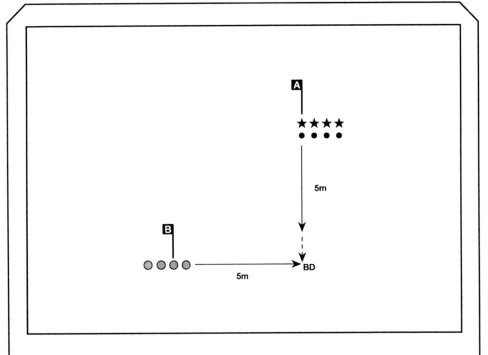

15. Blockdown From Different Angles:

1. Any number of players at A and B. One or more footballs at A.

2. A move forward to kick.

3. B move towards A and attempt blockdown.

4. A join B. B join A.

5. Drill continues.

6. **Variations:**

   1. Line A and B face each other

   2. A and B line up alongside each other.

   3. B chases from behind to block A.

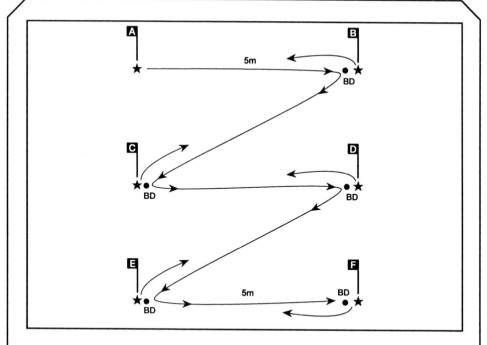

16. Pressure Blockdown:

1. One player at A, B, C, D, E and F, each with a football, except player at A.

2. A run to each player in turn and attempt to block their kicks.

3. After their kick each player moves to the next station, B to A, C to B, D to C, E to D, F to E.

4. A join F.

5. Drill continues from A.

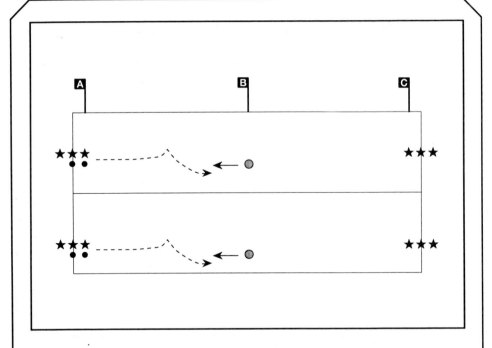

17. All Defensive Skills:

1.　Three or more players at A and C, 30m apart. Defender at B. One or more footballs at A.

2.　A attempts to move towards and kick to C. B uses all defensive skills to dispossess and/or blockdown.

3.　A join C. C repeats from this end.

4.　Rotate defensive player.

5.　Drill continues.

~ INDIVIDUAL ATTACKING SKILLS ~

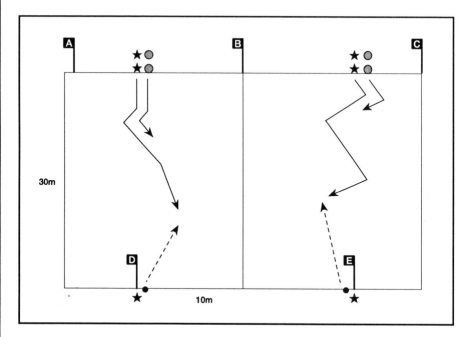

I. Get Free to Receive Drill:

1. Four or more players, working in pairs, at AB and BC. One player with a football, at D and E, who acts as a feeder.

2. Attacking player gets free of the defending player using any of the following moves:

   a) Change of pace.
   b) Change of direction.
   c) Run, check, run again.
   d) Run, check, go behind the defender.

3. Players return ball to D and E and rejoin their group.

4. Drill continues.

5. **Variation:** Add more players at D and E, working in pairs as defenders and attackers.

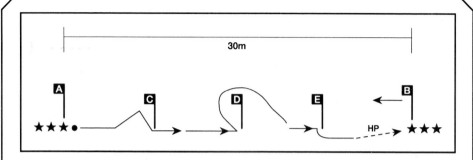

2. Triple Move Drill:

1. Three players or more at A and B. One football at A. Cones at C, D and E.

2. A run forward, sidestep at C, spin turn at D, and dummy solo at E. Pass to B. Join B.

3. B repeats from this end.

4. Practice moves on both sides of the body.

5. Drill continues.

6. **Variation:** Introduce defender at C, D and E.

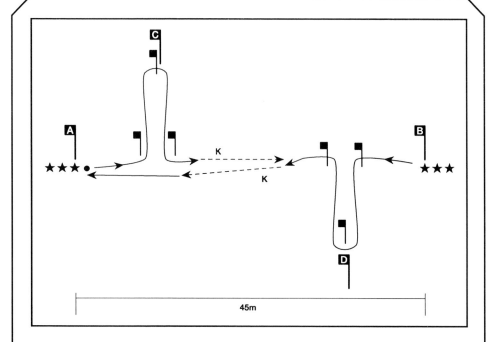

3. Evade and Get Free:

1. Three or more players at A and B. One football at A. Cones arranged as shown at C and D.

2. A, with ball, and B, without ball, begin together, going around cones at C and D respectively.

3. A kick to B. Join B.

4. B receives and kicks to next player at A. Join A.

5. Drill continues.

6. **Variation:** B soloes to C, going around the cones at C and handpasses to A.

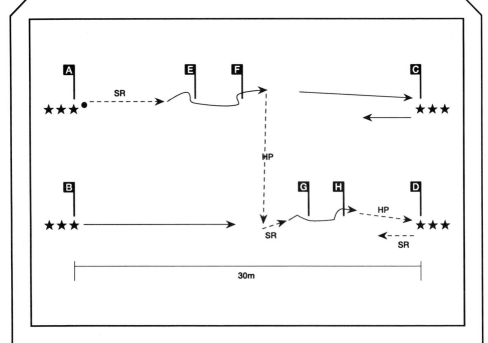

4. Evade and Support Drill:

1. Three or more players at A, B, C and D. Cones at E, F, G and H. One football at A.

2. A soloes and evades at E and F. B moves in support in the direction of G at the same time. A hand pass to B at G. Join C.

3. B soloes and evades at G and H. Pass to D. Join D.

4. D repeats from this end simultaneously with C.

5. Drill continues.

6. **Variation:** Introduce defender at E and H.

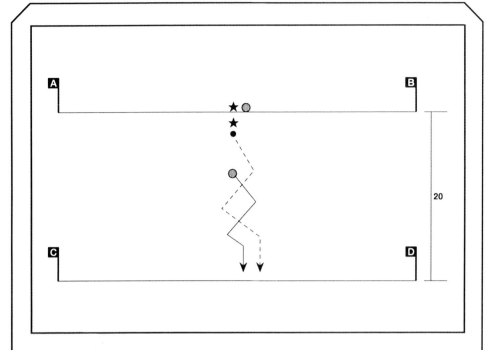

5. One on One:

1. Six to eight players working in pairs, as attackers and defenders at AB. One or more footballs.

2. Attacker, using any evasion skill of his choice, attempts to beat defender to reach CD. Remain at CD.

3. Drill continues with next pair.

4. Repeat from CD. Reverse roles.

5. **Variation:** Defenders apply token pressure only at first, progressing to full pressure as the drill continues.

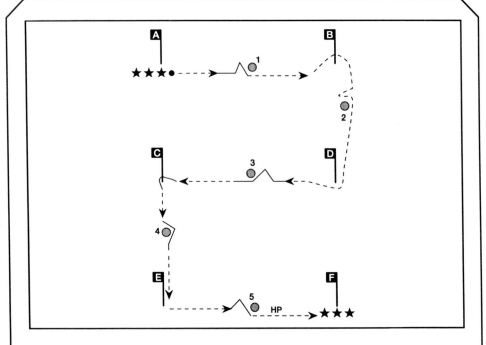

6. Beat the Man in the Middle:

1. Three or more players at A and F. Cones at B, C, D and E, all cones 10m apart. Defenders at 1, 2, 3, 4 and 5 arranged as shown. One football at A.

2. A moves towards B, evading defender 1 who offers token resistance. A continues through B, C, D and E, evading each defender in turn. Pass to F.

3. F repeats from this end.

4. Drill continues.

5. **Variation:**

    1. Any number of players at A only, each with a football.

    2. Same drill, but now the defenders apply full pressure.

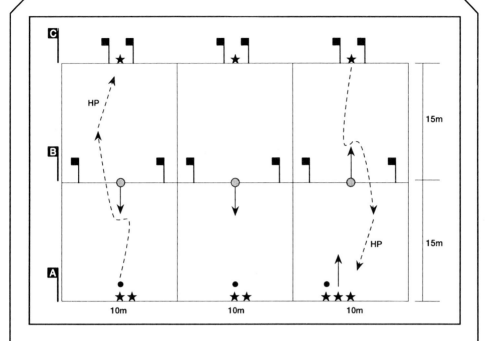

7. Through the Cones:

1. Arrange players in groups of four as shown in line A, B and C, three attacking players and one defender. One football at A.

2. A attacks the defender B, who leaves his line to meet him. A attempts to evade B and go through the cones.

3. When A has crossed the line at B, pass to C who repeats the drill from this end.

4. C pass to A.

5. Drill continues.

6. Rotate defensive player regularly.

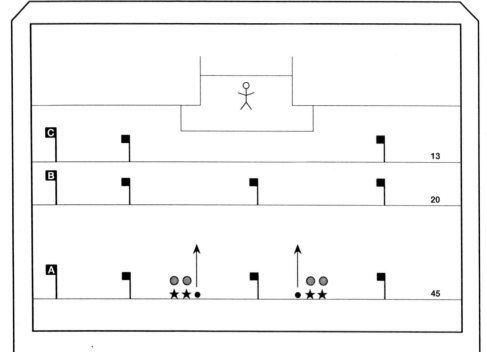

8. Beat me if you can:

1.   Any number of defenders and attackers at A (45m line). One football per pair. Goalkeeper on his line.

2.   Attackers attempt to evade defenders between A & B.

3.   If successful, A shoots for a goal between B and C (20-13m). Recover ball and rejoin A.

4.   If defender disposseses the attacking player both players rejoin A.

5.   Drill continues. Reverse roles.

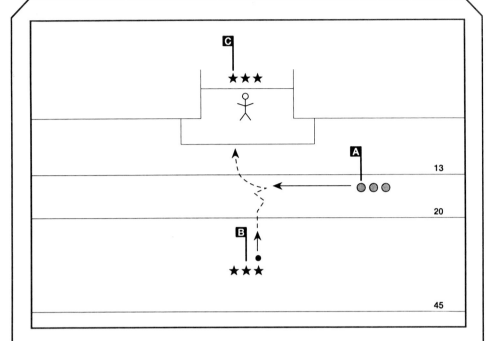

9. Go to Goal:

1. Three players or more at A, B and C. A act as defenders. One or more footballs at B. Goalkeeper on his line.

2. B attacks, A defends. B attempts to evade A and score a goal.

3. After his shot, B join C. A join B.

4. C recover ball and deliver to B. Join A.

5. Drill continues.

6. **Variation:** Introduce a condition limiting the number of solos/hops allowed to B.

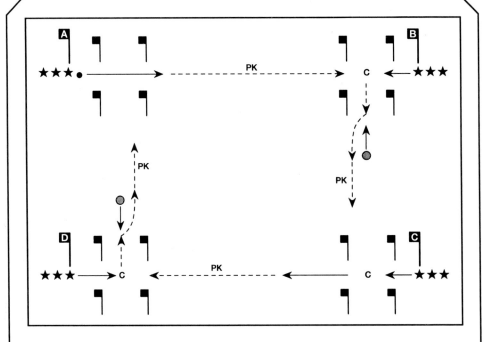

10. Receive, Evade and Pass Drill:

1. Arrange four grids as shown. Three or more players positioned outside each grid. One or more footballs at A. Defenders are placed close to grid B and D.

2. A kicks to B who runs to receive in Grid B. A join B.

3. As B turns to move in the direction of C, defender O exerts pressure immediately. B evades O and kicks or passes to C. B join C.

4. C kicks to D and joins D.

5. D, as at B, must evade defender O and pass or kick to A. Join A.

6. Drill continues. Rotate defenders.

7. **Variation:** Introduce defenders between AB and CD.

~ COMBINATION DRILLS ~
Scoring Drills

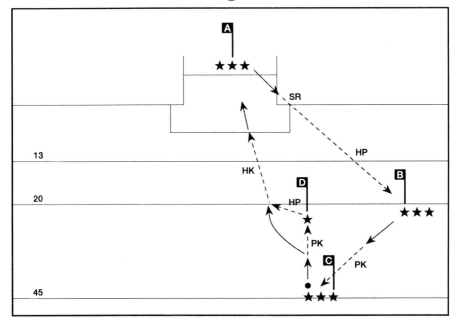

1. Kick, Receive and Score:

1. Three or more players at A,B and C, and one player at D. One or more footballs.

2. C kick to D, run on, receive return pass. Kick for score. Join A.

3. A recover ball, solo to and pass to B. Join B.

4. B kick to C. Join C

5. Drill continues

6. **Variation:**

    1. Player at D turn and shoot. Join A. Replace D with C.

    2. Add defender at D.

    3. Set up the drill on the left side.

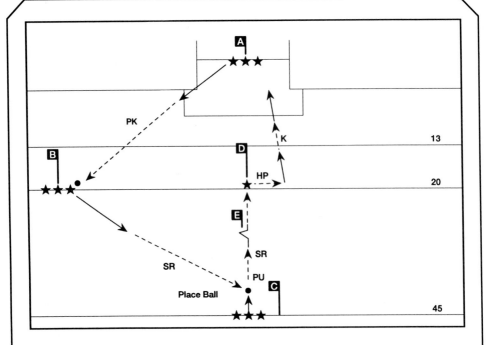

2. Five Skills Scoring Drill:

1. Three or more players at A, B and C. One stationary player at D. Cone at E. One football on the 45m line at C, one or more footballs at B.

2. C pick up, solo, sidestep at E, kick to D, take return pass, shoot for a score. Join A.

3. A kick to B. Join B.

4. B solo to C and place ball on the ground at the 45m line. Join C.

5. Drill continues.

6. **Variation:** Introduce a goalkeeper.

88

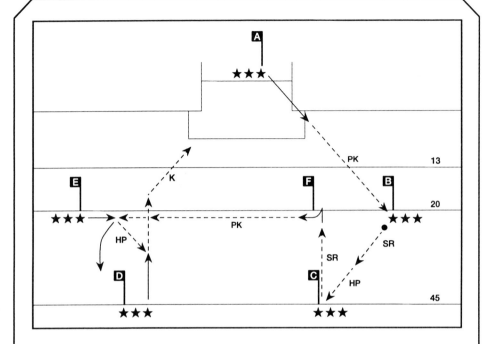

3. Switch the Play Drill:

1. Three players or more at A, B, C, D and E. Two or more footballs at B. Cone at F.

2. B solo and pass to C. Join C.

3. C solo to F. Practice an evasion move - sidestep, spin turn, dummy solo. Kick to E. Join E.

4. E pass to D on the burst. Join D.

5. D kicks for a score. Join A.

6. A kicks to B. Join B.

7. Drill continues.

8. **Variation:**

   1. Introduce defender between C and F.

   2. Introduce a goalkeeper.

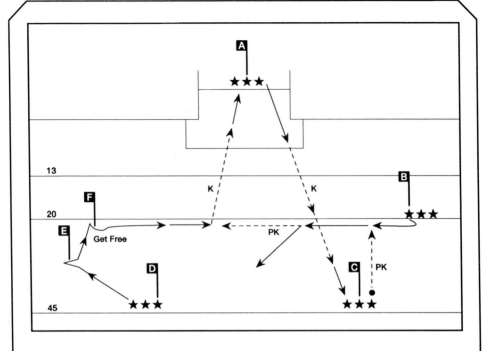

4. Get Free, Receive and Score:

1. Three or more players at A, B, C and D. Cones at E and F. One or more footballs at C.

2. C kick to B, who runs into position for the pass. Join B.

3. B kick to D, who times his run, evading an imaginary marker at E and F. Join D.

4. D kick for a score. Join A.

5. A kick long to C. Join C.

6. Drill continues.

7. **Variation:** Introduce defender at F.

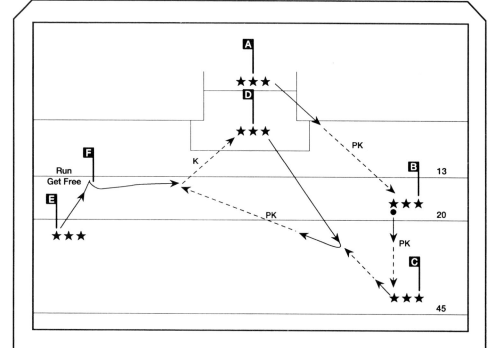

5. Wing to Centre to Wing Drill:

1. Three or more players at A, B, C, D and E. Cone at F. One or more footballs at B.

2. B kick to C. Join C.

3. C kick to D, who breaks from goal to get free. Join D.

4. D turns and sends a low pass to E who has eluded his marker at F. Join E.

5. F collects and scores. Join A.

6. A kick to B. Join B.

7. Drill continues.

8. **Variation:**

   1) Introduce defender at D.

   2) Intoduce goalkeeper.

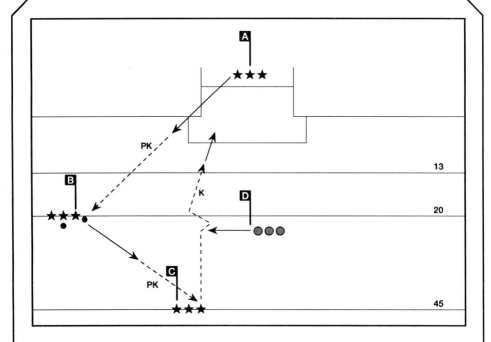

6. Beat the Man and Score:

1. Three players at A, B, C and D. Two or more footballs at B.

2. B kick to C. Join C.

3. C attacks the goal looking for a score. Players at station D act as defenders, who attempt to dispossess or block C.

4. After his scoring attempt, C Join A. D returns to his own line.

5. A retrieve ball, kick to B. Join B.

6. Drill continues. Rotate defensive players.

7. **Variation:**

   1) Introduce a goalkeeper.

   2) Organise same drill on the other wing.

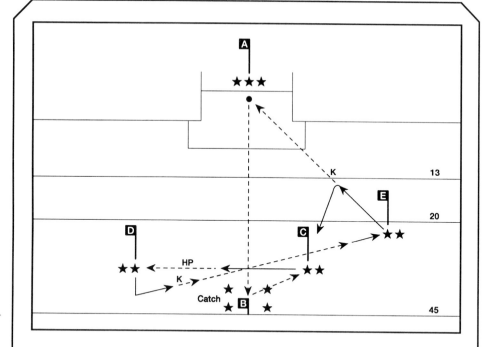

7. Goal to Centre to Wing:

1. Position defenders at A, midfielders at B. Two or more players at C,D and E. (wingbacks, forwards) One or more footballs at A.

2. A kicks long to centre, where B contest for high catch. If successful, pass to C. If the ball breaks, C should collect the ball.

3. C pass to D. Join D.

4. D kicks to the opposite wing, E. Join E.

5. E shoots for a score. Join C.

6. A return ball to B.

7. Drill continues.

8. **Variation:** Introduce defender at E.

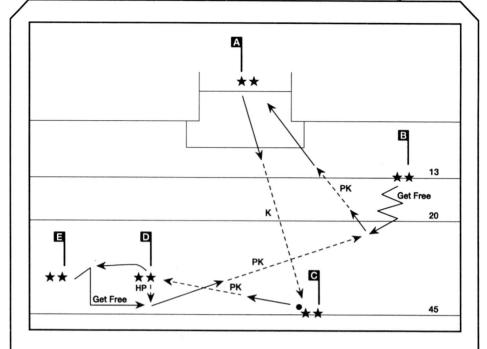

8. Wing to Opposite Corner:

1. Two players or more at each station A to E. One or more footballs at C.

2. C kick to D. Join D.

3. D pass to E who breaks to receive. D join E.

4. E kick to B, who breaks free, takes the ball and scores. E join B. B join A.

5. A kicks long to C. Join C.

6. Drill continues.

7. **Variation:** Introduce defender at E and B.

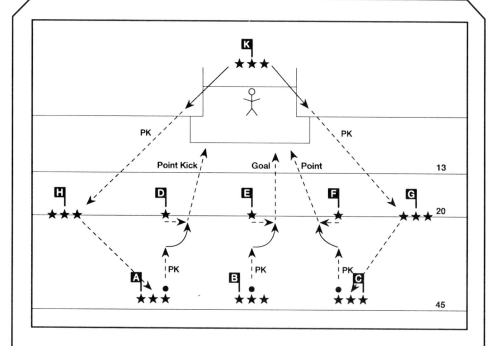

9. Target Practice Drill:

1.   Three or more players at A, B and C. Stationary players at D, E and F.
     Receivers at K, G and H. One or more footballs at A, B and C.
     Goalkeeper on his line.

2.   A, B and C kick to D, E and F, run on, take return pass and shoot for a
     score. B shoots for goal, A and C for points. Join K.

3.   K kick to H and G. Follow the kick and join H and G.

4.   G and H feed A, B and C.

5.   Drill continues.

6.   **Variation:**

     1. Introduce defender at E.

     2. Introduce defender at D and F.

~ PICK UP DRILLS ~

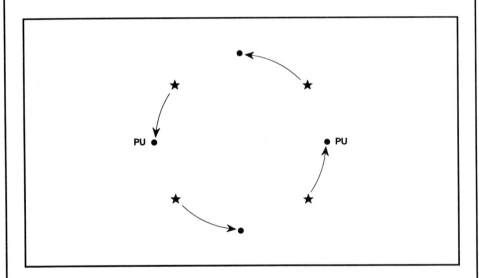

A. Stationary Ball

1. Circle Pick Up:

1.   Any number of players arranged in a circle. Suitable number of footballs.

2.   Players move around the circle. Pick and replace.

3.   Drill continues.

4.   Change direction. Change feet.

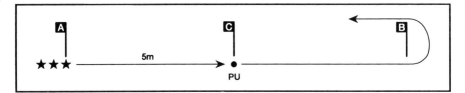

2. Pick and Replace:

1. Three or more players at A. One football at C. Cone at B.

2. A run to the ball at C: pick and replace: run around B and join A.

3. Next player repeats.

4. Drill continues.

5. **Variation:**

   1) A run, pick at C, replace, run around B and pick with opposite leg on return.

   2) Place three or more players at B. A run, pick and replace as before. Join B. B run, pick and replace. Join A.

   3) Drill continues.

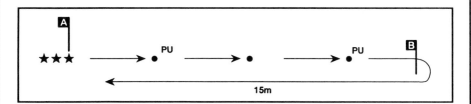

3. Relay Pick Up:

1. Three or more players at A. Three or more footballs between A and B. Cone at B.

2. In relay manner players at A move to each football in turn to pick and replace.

3. Run around B and return to A.

4. Drill continues.

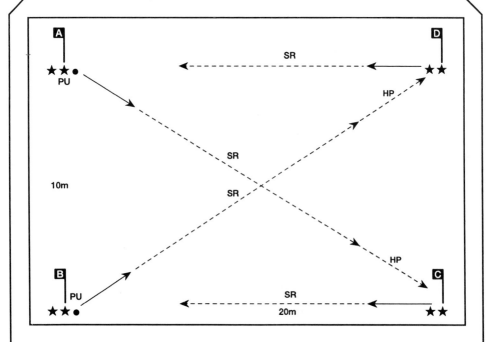

4. Pick and Solo:

1. Two players or more at A, B, C and D. One football at A and B.

2. A and B pick up the football simultaneously. A solo to C, pass to C and join C. B solo to D, pass to D, and join D.

3. D solo to A, place football on the ground at A. Join A.

4. C solo to B, place football on the ground at B. Join B.

5. Drill continues.

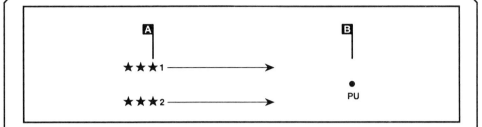

5. One on One Drill:

1. Four or more players working in pairs. One football at B, 5-10m from A.

2. First pair run to the ball to pick up. Token pressure only is exerted as player 1 picks and replaces.

3. Rejoin A. Next pair repeat.

4. Drill continues. Reverse roles.

5. **Variation:** Player 1 and 2 exert full pressure as they contest the ball.

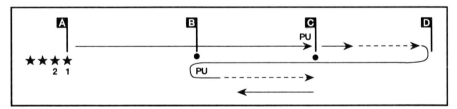

6. Shuttle Pick Up:

1. Three or more players at A. One football at B and C. Cone at D, 20m from A.

2. A1 pick up at C: replace at D. A1 then pick up at B and replace at C. Join A.

3. Player 2 at A pick up at C, replace at B. Pick up at D and replace at C. Join A.

4. Drill continues.

5. **Variation:** Use as a relay competition between different groups. Specify number of repetitions.

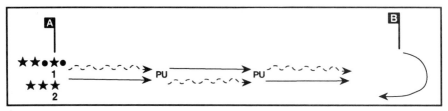

Rolling Ball - Away from the Player

I. Roll and Follow:

1. Three or more players at A, each with a football. Cone at B.

2. Player 1 rolls ball, chases and picks up. Continue around Cone B. Repeat. Join A.

3. Drill continues with next player.

4. **Variation:** Arrange players in pairs at A. Each player rolls the ball in turn for his partner who picks.

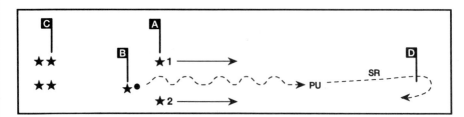

2. First to Pick:

1. Six or more players, working in pairs at C. One player with a football at B. Cones at A and D.

2. B rolls ahead between A1 and A2 who contest the pick up. Successful player solo and handpass to B. Join C.

3. Next pair at C repeat.

4. Exert token pressure only at first. Then apply full pressure.

5. Alternate roles. Rotate player B.

6. Drill continues.

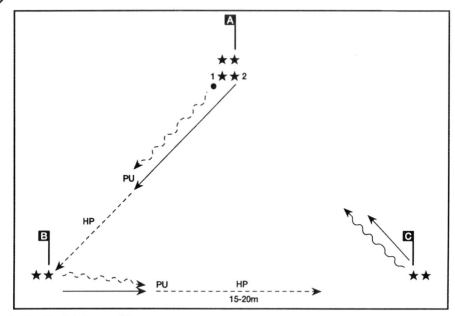

3. Roll, Pick and Pass:

1. Eight players, four at A, two at B and C. One football at A.
2. Moving in pairs, A1 rolls for A2 who picks and passes to B1. Join B.
3. B1 repeats for B2, who passes to C. Join C.
4. Drill continues in this manner. Alternate roles.

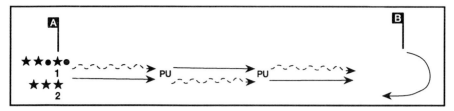

4. Roll and Pick:

1. Six or more players, acting in pairs, at A. Cone at B. One or more footballs.
2. Player 1 rolls football ahead of player 2. Player 2 picks and rolls for player 1.
3. Continue around cone B and rejoin A.
4. Drill continues.

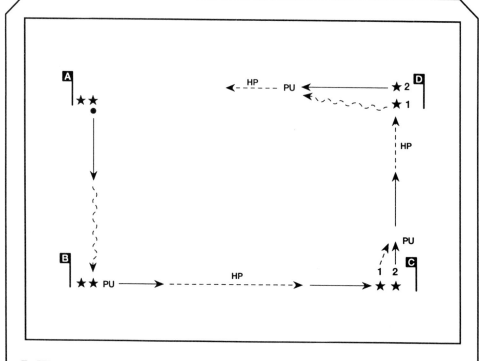

5. Three Pick Up Drill:

1. Two or more players at A, B, C and D. One football at A.

2. A roll to B. Join B. B pick, turn and pass to C1. Join C.

3. C1 places ball on the ground. C2 pick and pass to D1. Join D.

4. D1 roll ahead of D2 who picks and passes to A. Join A.

5. Drill continues.

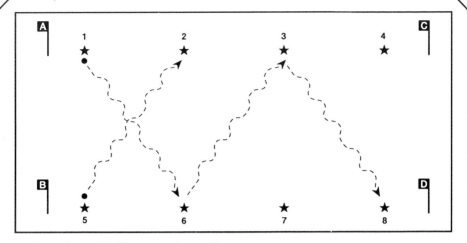

B. Rolling Ball - to the player

I. Over and Back:

1. Four or more players between cones at AC and BD. One football at A and B (Player 1 and 5).

2. Player 1 at A begins by rolling to player 6 at B, who picks and rolls to player 3.

3. Player 5 at B rolls to player 2, who picks and rolls to player 7.

4. Drill continues with ball going from 3 to 8, 8 to 3, 3 to 6 etc, and 7 to 4, 7 to 2 etc.

2. Meet and Pick:

1. Three or more players at A. One stationary player at B with a football.

2. B rolls to A1 and A2 who contest the pick up. Pass to B. Rejoin A.

3. Exert token pressure at first and full pressure later.

4. Drill continues.

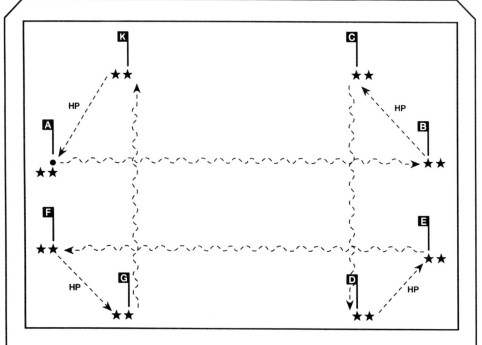

3. Pick and Pass:

1. Two or more players at each station, A to K. One football at A.

2. A roll to B. Join B.

3. B pick and pass to C. Join C.

4. C roll to D. Join D.

5. D pick and pass to E. Join E.

6. Drill continues in this manner.

7. **Variation:**

    1) Increase distance and use the kick.

    2) Player work in pairs at B, D, F and C and contest the pick up.

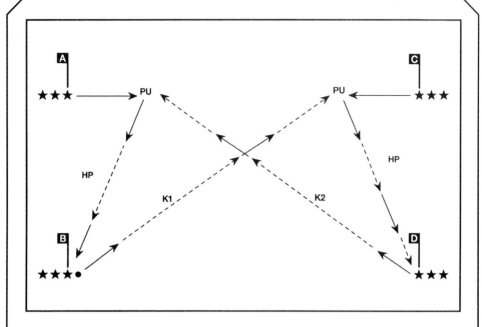

4. Kick, Pick and Pass Drill:

1.   Three or more players at A, B, C and D. One football at B.

2.   B kick low to C, who moves forward to meet the ball. B join C.

3.   C picks and handpasses to D. Join D.

4.   D kicks low to A, moving forward. Join A.

5.   A picks and handpasses to B. Join B.

6.   Drill continues.

~ COMBINATION DRILLS ~
Line Drills & Skill Circuit

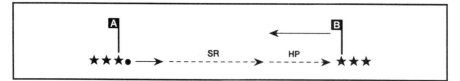

I. Solo, Pass and Catch:

1. Three or more players at A and B 30m apart. One football at A.
2. A soloes three times (optional). Pass high to B. Join B.
3. B makes an overhead catch and repeats.
4. Drill continues.
5. **Variation:**
    1) Use kickpass.
    2) Players work in pairs at A and B.

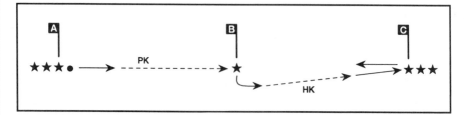

2. Kick, Catch and Kick Drill:

1. Three or more players at A and C, 40m apart. One player at B. One football at A.
2. A punt kicks to B. Join B.
3. B chest catches, turns and hook kicks to C. Join C.
4. C catches overhead and punts to B. Join B.
5. Drill continues.
6. **Variation:** Introduce defender at B.

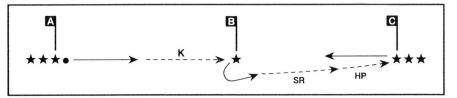

3. Kick, Solo and Pass:

1. Three or more players at A and C, 40m apart. One player at B. One football at A.

2. A kicks to B. Join B. B turns, soloes and passes to C. Join C.

3. C repeats.

4. Drill continues.

5. **Variation:**

   1) A pass to B, run, take return, solo and pass to C. Join C.
   2) Introduce defender at B.

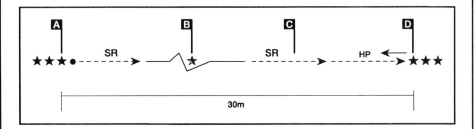

4. Solo, Evade and Pass Drill:

1. Three or more players at A and D. One defending player at B. One football at A. Cone at C.

2. A solo to B, beat the defender between B and C, solo and handpass to D. The defender offers token opposition only at first.

3. D repeats.

4. Drill continues. Rotate defender.

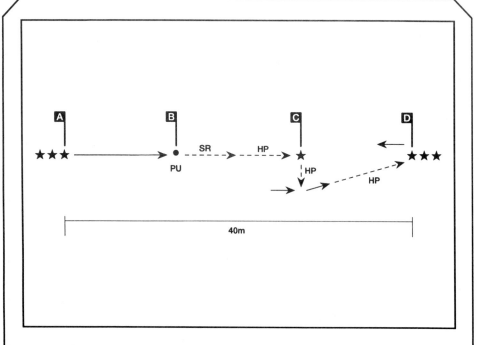

5. Pick, Solo, Pass and Catch:

1. Three or more players at A and D. One stationary player at C. One football at Cone B.

2. A run: pick up: solo: pass to C: take return at chest height: pass high to D. Join D.

3. D catches overhead: solo: pass to C: take return at chest height: solo: place ball at B. Join A.

4. Drill continues.

5. **Variation:**

   1) Player at C moves on receipt of pass. Replace with the player who makes the pass.

   2) Introduce defender at C.

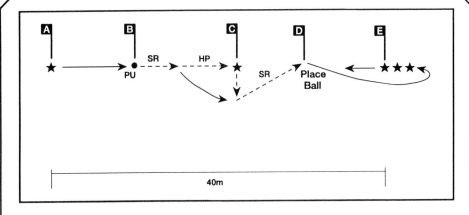

6. Pick, Pass and Solo Drill:

1. Three or more players at A and D. One stationary player at C. Cones at B and D. One football at B.

2. A run to B: pick up: solo: pass to C: take return: solo to D: place ball on the ground at D. Join E.

3. C returns, performing the same skills.

4. Drill continues.

5. **Variation:**

    1) Player at C moves. Replace with A or E

    2) Introduce defender at C.

7. All Skills Pair Drill:

1. Arrange players in pairs, 10 - 20m apart. One football between four.

2. A kicks to B, who contest the ball. All skills may be practiced - overhead catch, low catch, hook kicks, punt kicks, block down etc.

3. Drill continues with the coach calling instructions.

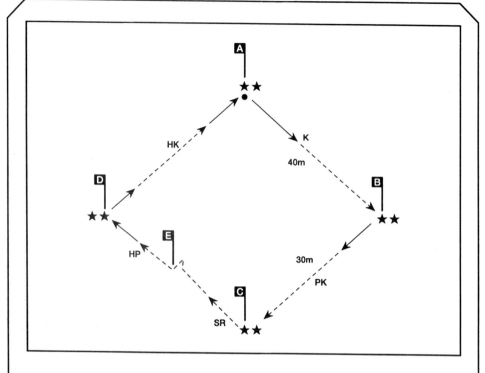

8. All Skills Diamond Drill:

1. Two or more players at A, B, C and D. Cone at E. One football at A.

2. A kick long to B. Join B.

3. B catch; punt to C. Join C.

4. C catch; solo: evade cone at E: pass to D. Join D.

5. D hook kicks to A. Join A.

6. Drill continues.

7. **Variation:** Introduce defender at E.

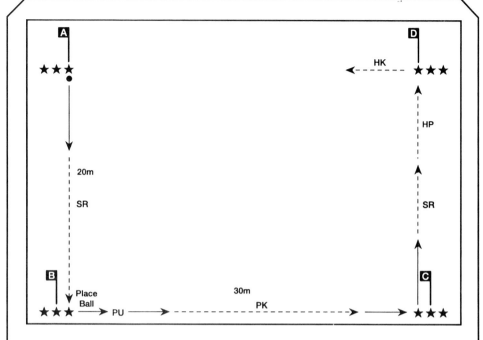

9. Pick, Kick, Solo and Pass:

1. Three or more players at A, B, C and D. One or more footballs at A.

2. A solo to B. Place football on the ground. Join B.

3. B pick up and punt kick to C. Join C.

4. C catch, solo and handpass to D. Join D.

5. D hook kicks to A. Join A.

6. Drill continues.

7. **Variation:** Introduce defender at A and C.

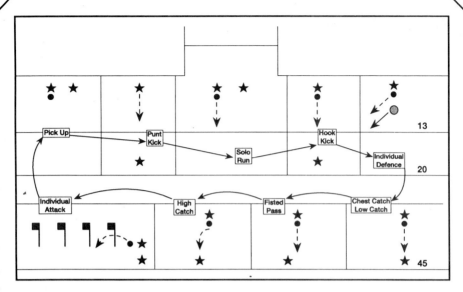

10. Skill Circuit:

1. Pick Up
2. Punt Kick
3. Solo Run
4. Hook Kick
5. Individual Defence
6. Chest Catch / Low Catch
7. Fisted Pass
8. High Catch
9. Individual Attack

1. Arrange circuit as suggested in the diagram.
2. Players work in pairs, two or more at each station. One football per pair.
3. Players practice each skill for a specified time or a specified number of attempts.
4. On the coach's whistle, players move to the next station.
5. Drill continues.

~ GOALKEEPING DRILLS ~

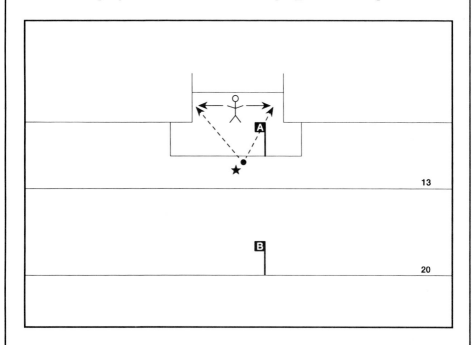

I. One to One:

1. Two players with the goalkeeper on his line and the other player at A. One football at A.

2. A throws the ball at different heights, angles, speed to the facing goalkeeper who reacts and saves.

3. **Variation:** Goalkeeper turns his back to player A. A calls, goalkeeper turns, A throws.

4. Player at A moves to cone B and kicks for goal. Goalkeeper reacts to attempt save.

5. Goalkeeper may face the player, or turn his back, as in variation at 3 above.

6. Drill continues.

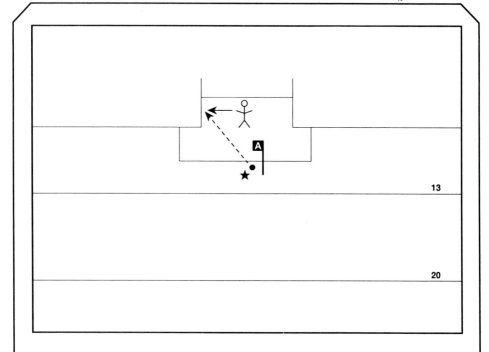

2. Reflex Reaction:

1. Goalkeeper kneels on the ground on the goaline. Player at A with one football.

2. A throws the ball at different angles, heights and speed to the goalkeeper who attempts the save.

3. **Variations:**

   1) Player lies on his stomach. A calls, goalkeeper responds by rising and readying himself for the shot. A throws and goalkeeper attempts save.

   2) Same drill with goalkeeper on his back.

   3) Place player A on 20m line and repeat with A kicking for goal.

4. Drill continues.

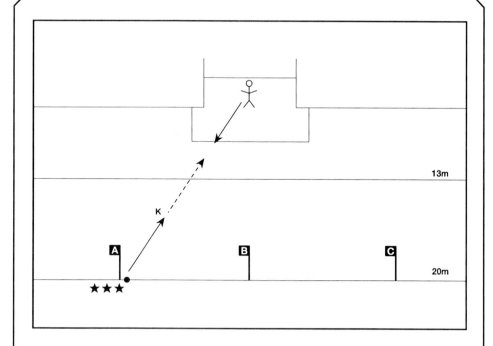

3. Narrow the Angle:

1. Three players or more at A. Goalkeeper on his line. Two or more footballs at A.

2. A moves with the ball towards goal, to shoot from the 13m line.

3. Goalkeeper advances to narrow shooting angle.

4. A kicks. Goalkeeper attempts save. A retrieve ball.

5. Drill continues.

6. **Variation:**

    1) Introduce a new group of players, or rotate players from A, to cone B and/or Cone C.

    2) Rotate goalkeepers.

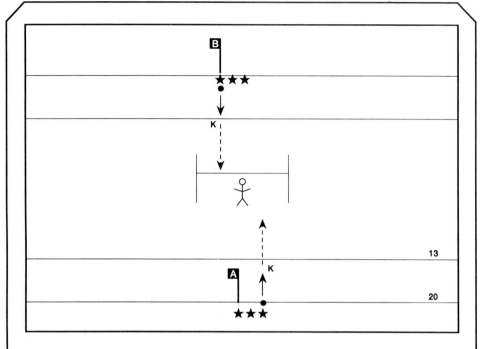

4. Goalie in the Middle:

1. Three or more players at A and B, 20m in front and behind goal. (Use portable goal or cones) Two or more footballs at A and B. Goalkeeper on his line.

2. A shoots for goal; goalkeeper attempts save. If goalkeeper is successful A retrieves ball and rejoins A. If shooter is successful B retrieves ball.

3. B now shoots from the other side. Goalkeeper attempts save. B rejoin B

4. Drill continues with alternate shots from A and B.

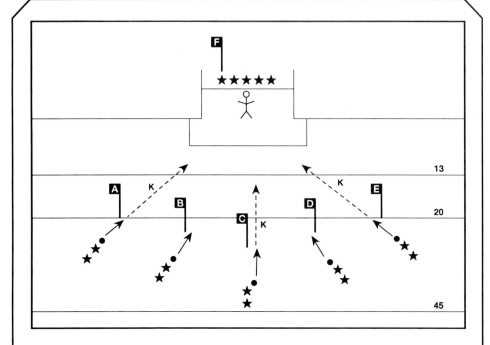

5. Pressure Save Drill:

1. Players work in threes. Any number of stations, 3 - 5 as appropriate. One football at each station. Players line up 10m from the cones at A, B, C, D and E.

2. A runs to and shoots at Cone A. Immediately after A shoots, B begins his run to shoot at Cone B. C then begins his run to shoot at Cone C. D and E repeat process.

3. After their shot A, B, C, D and E join F.

4. Players at F retrieve ball and return to shooting lines at A, B, C, D and E respectively.

5. Drill continues.

6. **Variation:** Place a stationery player at each cone. Shooters kick to this player, take return and shoot.

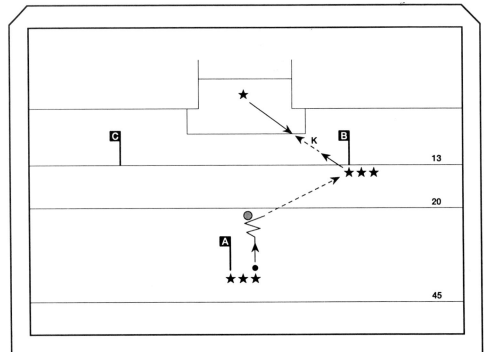

6. Only the Goalie to Beat:

1. Three players or more at A and B. Goalkeeper on his line. Two or more footballs at A. Defender on 20m line.

2. A solo and try to evade defender. A pass to B and join B.

3. B must shoot. Goalkeeper advances to block attempted shot. B retrieves ball and joins A.

4. Drill continues. Rotate defender.

5. **Variation:**

    1) Introduce players at cone C (3 V 1)

    2) Introduce two defenders (3 V 2).

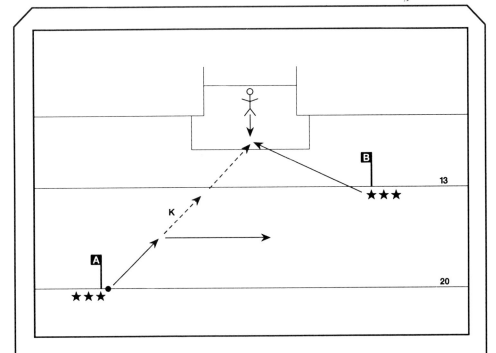

7. Catch or Punch:

1. Three or more players at A and B. Two or more footballs at A. Goalkeeper on his line.

2. A kicks the ball to land in the area of the small square. A join B.

3. B runs in to challenge goalkeeper for the ball.

4. Goalkeeper decides to catch or punch clear.

5. B retrieves ball. Join A.

6. **Variation:** B becomes the kicking line.

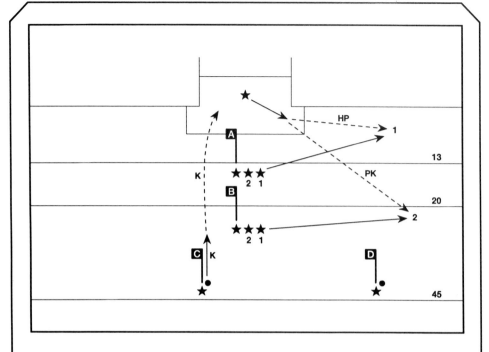

8. Catch and Clear:

1. Goalkeeper on his line, three or more players at A and B. One player at C and D, with a football each.

2. Player at C or D kick high to the goalkeeper who catches in the square. He immediately breaks with the ball to the left or to the right.

3. Player 1 at A and B respond by breaking to the same side to receive from the goalkeeper, who is presented with two options: 1) handpass to A in the corner back position or: 2) kick to B in the half-back position.

4. The ball is returned to C or D through these players, who either kick directly to C and D or interchange passes and support each other. A and B rejoin their own line.

5. Player at C or D repeat kick to the goalkeeper and the drill continues.

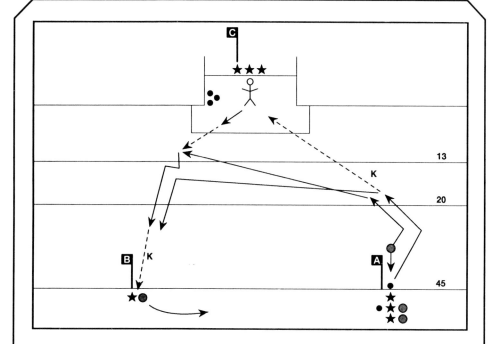

9. Stop and Restart:

1. Arrange any number of players at A and B. Three players at C. Players work in pairs, one defender, one attacker. Two or more footballs at A and three footballs in the goals at C.

2. Attacking player at A tries to evade the defender and shoots for goal between the 13m and 20m line. Goalkeeper attempts to save.

3. Immediately after the shot the defender runs to receive pass from the goalkeeper inside the 13m line. The defender must evade the attacker and deliver the ball to the next pair at B. A join B.

4. B join F.

5. Next pair at A repeat.

6. Drill continues. Players at C return the ball to the goalkeeper. Rotate after specified time.

~ PENALTY KICK DRILLS ~

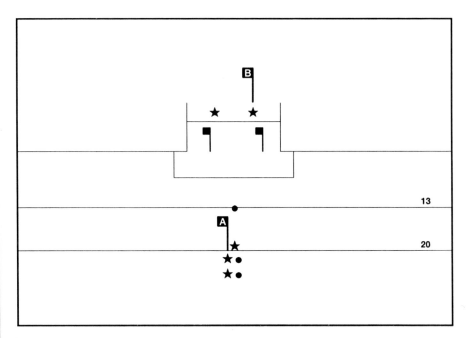

I. Inside the Post Drill:

1.   Arrange cones 1m inside each goalpost. Arrange penalty kickers at A with a football each. Two or more players at B.

2.   Player 1 place ball on 13 metre line. Direct the ball low between the cone and the post. Players at B retrieve the ball.

3.   Player 2 repeats.

4.   Continue drill for a specified number of attempts.

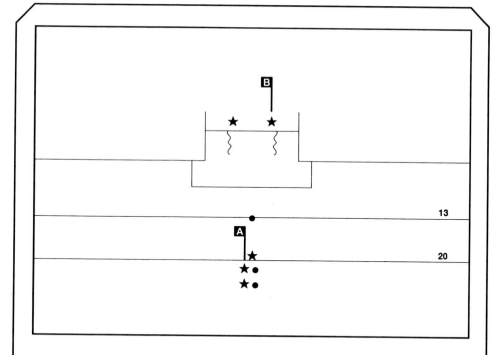

2. Top Corner Drill:

1.   Tie a piece of rope, a jersey or a tracksuit bottom onto the Crossbar, one metre inside the post. Arrange penalty kickers at A with a football each. Two or more players at B.

2.   Player 1 attempts penalty kick, directing the ball towards the top corner of his choice between the rope and the post. Players at B retrieve the ball.

3.   Player 2 repeats.

4.   Continue drill for a specified number of attempts.

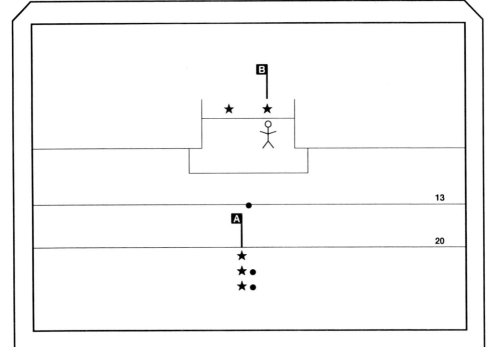

3. Open Goal Drill:

1. Goalkeeper positions himself close to post at any side. Penalty kickers at A, one football each. Two or more players at B.

2. Player 1 attempts penalty kick, directing the ball to the open side away from the goalkeeper who attempts to save. Goalkeeper or the players at B return ball to A.

3. Player 2 repeats.

4. Drill continutes.

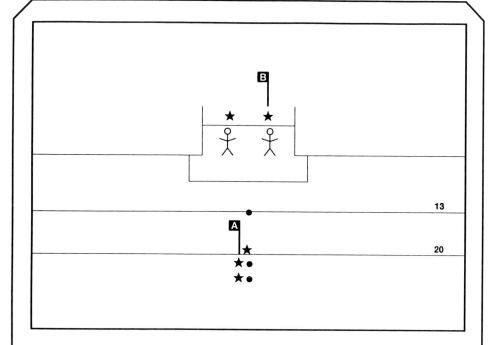

4. Pick your Spot:

1.   Place two goalkeepers on the goal line, in a stationary position. Penalty kickers at A.

2.   Player 1 attempts his kick, picking his spot between the goalkeepers, or between the goalkeeper and post. Goalkeepers are not allowed to move their feet. Successful attempts are counted. Goalkeepers or players at B return ball to A.

3.   Player 2 repeats.

4.   Drill continues.

5.   **Variations**:

   1) Place the two goalkeepers in the centre

   2) Allow free movement of the goalkeepers across the line.

   3) Use one goalkeeper only, after a specified time.

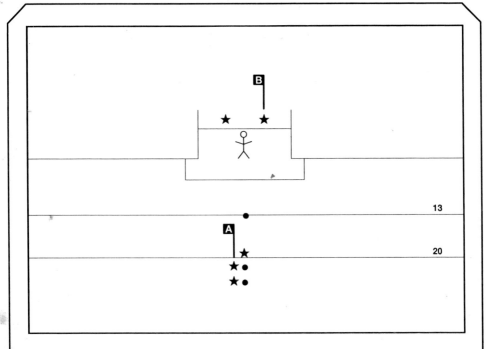

5. The Real Thing:

1. Goalkeeper on the goaline, penalty kickers at A with a football each. Two or more players at B.

2. A places the ball and takes his penalty kick. Goalkeeper attempts the save.

3. Next player repeats.

4. The goalkeeper or the players at B return the ball to A.

5. **Variation:** Include defenders and attackers on the 20 m line, ready for saves, rebounds and follow up shots.

~ FREE KICK DRILLS ~

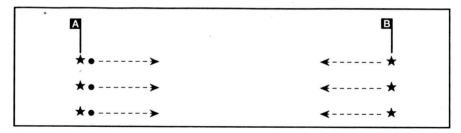

1. One to One Drill:

1. Arrange players in pairs at A and B, 20-40m apart. One football per pair.
2. A kicks to B. B catches, places ball and returns kick to A.
3. Drill continues for a specified time.
4. Vary distances between A and B.

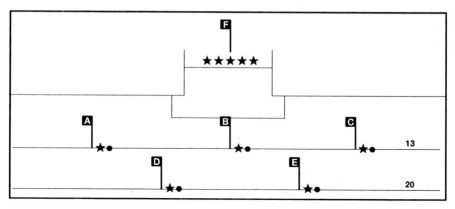

2. Close to Goal Technique Drill:

1. Arrange players in pairs. Freetakers at A, B, C, D and E with a football each and partners at F.
2. Players take specified number of frees, 5-10, from each position. Players at F recover the ball.
3. Reverse roles.
4. Drill continues.
5. **Variation:** Introduce competition.

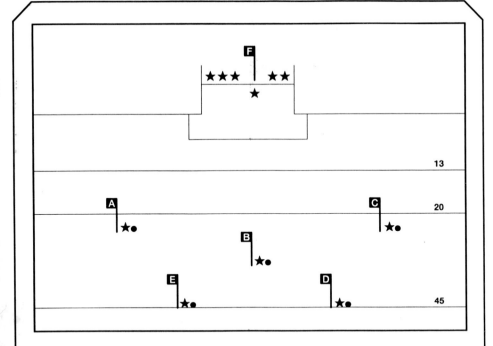

3. Distance and Accuracy Drill:

1. Arrange cones at random between 20m-45m line. Freetakers with a ball each at A, B, C, D and E. Goalkeeper and defenders at F.

2. Players take specified number of frees at each station, eg. 5.

3. Goalkeeper and defenders return the ball using free kicks only.

4. Drill continues.

5. **Variation:** Introduce competition.

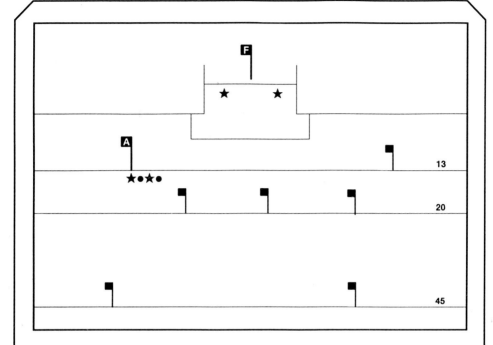

4. Sharpshooter Drill:

1. Arrange cones at random between 13m-45m line.

2. Arrange four players, one goalkeeper and one defender at F, and the top two freetakers on the 13m line at A. Four or more footballs required.

3. Freetaker No. 1 and No. 2 go head to head at each cone. Specify number of attempts at each cone or else the number of station circuits.

4. Players at F return the ball.

5. Record the results each time.

Sample Training Sessions using these drills

A typical training session will consist of five major components: the warm up; the drill section; the game or part of the game section: the specific fitness section; and the warm down.

The following are four sample sessions which serve as an example of how you can use this book to plan out the drill section of your training session, which normally would be of 20/25 minute duration.

SESSION I
SKILLS COVERED: *Kicking, Catching, Passing*

SESSION II
SKILLS COVERED: *Attacking Skills, Solo Run, Evasion, Kicking, Passing, Catching*

SESSION III

SKILLS COVERED: *Defensive Skills, Footwork, Flicking, Blockdown, Solo Run, Kicking, Catching, Attacking*

SESSION IV

Using a Drill Section to concentrate on one skill only – ie: the handpass

Remember that you can use drills from one section only or any possible number of combinations using the different drill sections when you plan your session. Enjoy yourself. It will be great fun and real easy to do!

HOW TO MAKE
— REALLY —
GOOD COFFEE

CONTENTS

GREEN BEANS

SEVERAL VARIETIES / ENDLESS POSSIBILITIES

Coffee is grown in tropical regions of the world with hot climates, high rainfall and good drainage.

The green bean is one of two seeds from the cherry (Fig. 1) of a coffee tree. A coffee tree takes four to five years to mature, after which it can produce enough cherries each year to yield approximately one kilogram of roasted coffee. There are two main species of coffee tree: *Coffea arabica* and *Coffea canephora*, commonly referred to as *robusta*.

Arabica

Arabica (Fig. 2) grows best at altitudes over 900 metres above sea level. It is widely believed that *arabica* beans produce a higher-quality coffee than other coffee species. *Arabica* coffee trees require certain conditions in order to flourish — weather, light and temperature are all important considerations. Specialty coffees are almost always *arabica*.

Robusta

As its name suggests, *robusta* is more resistant to disease and can grow at lower altitudes than *arabica*. It has an astringent flavour and much higher levels of caffeine. *Robusta* is often used in instant coffee as it is usually more economical.

There are a few very high-quality *robusta* coffees — these can be used in small percentages to improve the *crema* and body of espresso blends.

Fig. 1 The seven layers to a coffee cherry

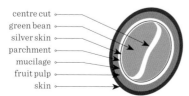

centre cut
green bean
silver skin
parchment
mucilage
fruit pulp
skin

The harvesting of coffee cherries differs by geographical location; most are picked by hand, some are picked using machines. The ripest fruit is selected first.

Processing

The green bean is extracted from the cherry. There are three main methods for processing, each of which has an effect on the flavour of the coffee: wet process; pulp natural or honey process; and dry process.

Wet process (washed coffee)

With the wet process, the skin and fruit pulp are removed from the cherry before the beans are soaked in water. This helps to remove the parchment and any impurities. The cherries are then dried (either in the sun or mechanically with large commercial driers), hulled and sorted.

Washed coffee beans command a premium because inferior beans can be identified and removed more readily by this method — resulting in a higher-quality 'cup'.

Washed coffee is usually clean and bright with a light body.

Pulp natural / honey process (semi-washed coffee)

With this process, the skin and fruit pulp are removed from the cherry. The beans are then dried with the parchment and a layer of mucilage intact, before being hulled and sorted.

The pulp natural process is said to round out the acidity and increase body.

Dry process (natural method)

First, in the natural method, the cherries are dried — typically on mats in the sun. When the pulp is completely dry, it is removed and the beans are then sorted.

Dry-processed green beans are usually sweeter with a heavier body, because of the extra time they have spent in contact with the fruit pulp.

Fig. 2 *Coffea arabica*

Sorting and grading

Green beans are graded and sorted by size then packed into sacks. L'affare uses only 100% top-graded green beans. We sample-roast and select on flavour and quality.

Decaffeinated coffee

Caffeine is a naturally occurring compound that is present in the leaves, seeds and fruits of more than 60 different plant species worldwide. Decaffeination is the process of removing the caffeine from these plants.

There are various methods of decaffeinating coffee, but at L'affare we favour the environmentally-friendly and chemical-free *Swiss Water Process*.

First, the green beans are cleaned and hydrated with water to prepare them for caffeine extraction. They are then soaked in water that has been saturated with green coffee extract (GCE). A carbon-filtering system continually traps caffeine until the beans are 99.9% caffeine free, the internationally recognised standard for decaffeinated coffee.

Sustainability

Sustainability is an important aspect of coffee production. The three key pillars of sustainability with relation to the coffee industry are:

- Environmental: improving the way coffee is produced by mitigating the impact of the production process on the environment;
- Economic: making the most efficient use of the resources available;
- Social: improving the lives of those involved in coffee production.

The primary sustainability certifications for coffee are Fairtrade, Rainforest Alliance and UTZ Certified.

Fairtrade

Fairtrade is an independent certification system that offers improved terms of trade for farmers and workers. It promotes fair prices and decent working conditions for sustainable producers in the developing world. An additional premium is offered for community projects or for investment into improving the productivity and quality of crops.

It is a unique system — farmers are joint partners in Fairtrade, with part ownership of the Fairtrade General Assembly, its governance body.

www.fairtrade.org.nz

Rainforest Alliance

Rainforest Alliance works to conserve biodiversity and ensure sustainable livelihoods by transforming land-use practices, business operations and consumer behaviour.

The Rainforest Alliance Certified™ seal is awarded to farms that meet comprehensive standards in environmental protection, worker welfare and best farming practices.

www.rainforest-alliance.org

UTZ Certified

UTZ Certified stands for sustainable farming and better opportunities for farmers, their families and the environment. UTZ develops sustainable supply chains for agricultural products that are transparent from farm to manufacturer.

Certified farms and businesses are closely monitored annually by independent third parties. They assure good agricultural practices and management, safe and healthy working conditions, no child labour and protection of the environment.

www.utzcertified.org

DID YOU KNOW?
'Fair Trade' is a broader term used to refer to the Fair Trade movement as a whole and is used to describe both goods that are independently certified and labelled with the Fairtrade mark and unlabelled, uncertified goods.

'Direct Trade' is an alternative label to describe the sourcing of coffee directly from farmers. Although there is no agreed definition of the term, it is seen as an alternative to Fairtrade certification but is not independently audited.

COFFEE-PRODUCING COUNTRIES

HOT, HIGH AND WET

If you want to know what coffee from a particular country tastes like, choose a 'single origin' — a coffee made from the beans of just one country, region, farm or micro-lot. The flavour of the coffee is influenced by the soil, climate and altitudes of each region.

A Brazil
Brazil is the world's largest coffee producer. The best Brazilian coffee is full-bodied, sweet and aromatic. It is an ideal base for espresso.

B Colombia
Most Colombian coffee is smooth and full-bodied, with complex acidity and rich flavour.

C Guatemala
Famed for their quality, top Guatemalan coffees have moderate acidity and excellent body.

D Honduras
Full-bodied, rich and earthy in flavour, Honduran beans have mild spice and undertones of chocolate.

E **Mexico**

Coffee from Mexico is often roasted to a slightly darker roast profile. It is usually mild, light-bodied and sweet.

F **Peru**

Peru is renowned for its high-quality beans which are mellow and mild — this makes them perfect for blending.

G **Ethiopia**

Ethiopia is the birthplace of coffee. Ethiopian beans tend to have fruity aroma and acidity, and are sweet and complex in flavour.

H **Kenya**

Much of Kenya's coffee is grown at high altitude on the slopes of Mount Kenya. It is flavourful with a deep winey acidity and a dry finish.

DID YOU KNOW?
India, Indonesia and Vietnam are also top coffee-producing countries, specialising primarily in *robusta* production. *Robusta* coffee currently accounts for around 20% of the world market.

PRINCIPAL CATEGORIES OF TASTING

IT'S ALL ABOUT FLAVOUR

SMELL

Fragrance — the smell of roasted coffee, prior to brewing.

Aroma — the smell of freshly brewed coffee.

TASTE

Acidity — the pleasant 'brightness' of a coffee. It is an indicator of both quality and altitude.

Flavour — the taste of the coffee once its aroma, acidity and body have been considered.

FEEL

Body — the texture and weight of the coffee in your mouth. A thin or light body can feel watery; full-bodied delivers a heavier mouthfeel. Think of it like trim milk versus full-fat cream.

Finish — the residual feeling in your mouth and aftertaste of the coffee.

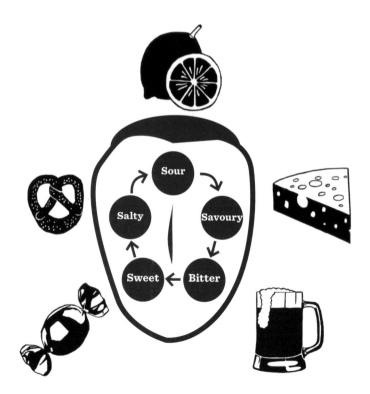

ROASTING

The majority of coffee companies use a drum roaster to roast their coffee. Hot air is passed through a rotating drum which continuously tumbles the green beans throughout the roasting cycle.

The cycle takes around 15 minutes. In that time the green bean will lose about 20% of its weight, expand in size by 30% and change colour to brown.

As moisture evaporates from within the beans, the cell walls break, making a distinctive noise known as the *first crack* (165–180°C). It is at this point that the roaster keeps a watchful eye on the changing colour of the beans to determine when the desired roast profile has been achieved. The complex sugars will start to caramelise and the flavour really begins to develop.

Soon after (195–220°C), there is a *second crack*. More than 1,000 chemical reactions will have taken place within the bean by this time.

Most roasters complete their roast between first and second crack. A slightly lighter roast is used when the roaster wants to retain more of the acidity and natural fruit flavour of the bean. A slightly darker roast profile will increase the body and sweetness of the coffee. Very dark roasts can have bitter, smoky and burnt characteristics.

Fig. 3 L'affare's Probat G120 coffee roaster

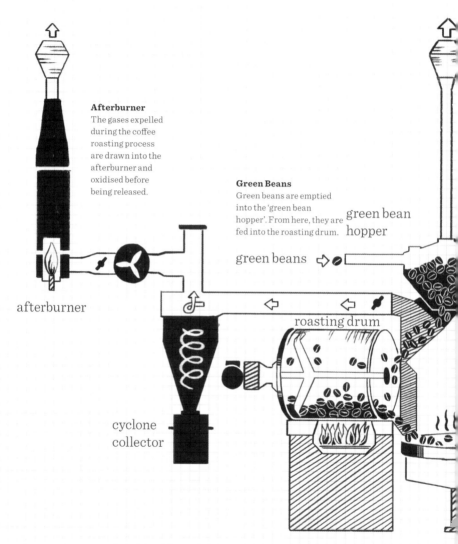

Afterburner
The gases expelled during the coffee roasting process are drawn into the afterburner and oxidised before being released.

Green Beans
Green beans are emptied into the 'green bean hopper'. From here, they are fed into the roasting drum.

green bean hopper

green beans

afterburner

roasting drum

cyclone collector

Roasting Drum
A flow of hot air is generated by a burner in a combustion chamber inside the base of the roaster. The air is circulated through the insulated chamber of the roasting drum. The drum rotates and is equipped with stirring paddles to ensure the beans are roasted evenly.

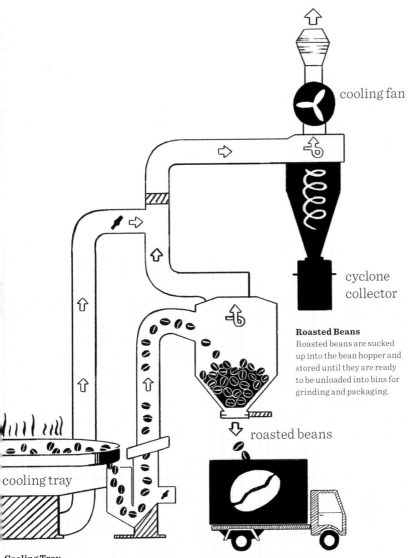

cooling fan

cyclone
collector

Roasted Beans
Roasted beans are sucked
up into the bean hopper and
stored until they are ready
to be unloaded into bins for
grinding and packaging.

roasted beans

cooling tray

Cooling Tray
When the beans reach the desired roast
profile, they are emptied into the cooling tray.
Here, the coffee is cooled by large mechanical
arms, which revolve and slowly move it
around the tray. Heat is drawn from the
beans and is cooled by an extractor located
underneath the perforated floor of the tray.

BLENDING

Combining two or more single-origin coffees together is called blending (Fig. 4). The aim is to combine coffees with complementary characteristics: for example, acid with sweet; thin-bodied with full-bodied.

At L'affare, we roast the green beans from each origin separately. Once they have been roasted, we combine the different origins to create blends that are balanced and complex in flavour. This process is known as post-blending.

Fig. 4 Example of a blend of beans

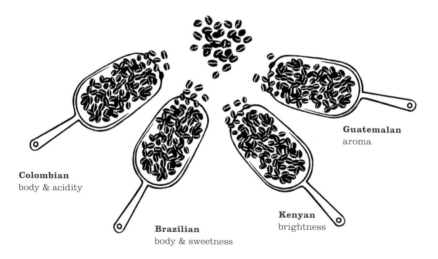

Guatemalan
aroma

Colombian
body & acidity

Brazilian
body & sweetness

Kenyan
brightness

STORAGE, PACKAGING & FRESHNESS

Good coffee must be served fresh — just how fresh depends on how well the coffee is stored. In a café environment, beans more than four weeks old will start to deteriorate and taste stale, dull and flat. Equally, beans used too soon after roasting can result in espresso that has bubbly crema and a tart flavour.

The lifecycle of your roasted coffee will depend on how well you look after it. Coffee should be stored in airtight packaging away from oxygen, light, moisture, extremes in temperature and strong smells that it may absorb.

For retail sales, we package our coffee in foil bags embedded with a one-way valve immediately after roasting. This prevents the beans from oxidising, as it allows the coffee's naturally occurring gases to escape from the bags without allowing oxygen in.

Coffee loses its flavour more quickly once it has been ground. Ideally, grind no more than you are going to consume. If you do not own a good *burr grinder,* try to purchase your coffee at least once a week.

PLUNGER COFFEE

A plunger might also be referred to as a *French press, cafetière* or *press pot*.

1. Place medium-ground/plunger-grind coffee into the plunger pot, one tablespoon (15g) of coffee per 250ml cup.

2. Bring freshly drawn water to the boil and allow it to cool for 30 seconds so the temperature drops to between 92°C and 96°C.

3. Slowly pour hot water onto the coffee grounds. You should only add enough water to ensure the grounds are wet. This allows the coffee to *bloom*, opening up and releasing its unique flavours.

4. Once the coffee has stopped bubbling and the bloom is complete, slowly pour the remaining hot water onto the grounds. Stir briefly.

5. Place the plunger on top of the pot. Allow four minutes of infusion time before plunging.

AEROPRESS

There are a few alternative ways to brew coffee using an Aeropress. We have explained two of the more popular methods below.

Method 1 — Traditional

1. Remove the plunger from the chamber and set it aside.

2. Remove the filter cap from the chamber and insert a paper filter into it. Replace the cap.

3. Sit the chamber on top of your cup or server and, using the Aeropress scoop, add one level scoop (13g) of medium-ground, plunger- or filter-grind coffee into the chamber per 200ml of water.

4. Bring freshly drawn water to the boil and allow it to cool for 30 seconds so the temperature drops to between 92°C and 96°C.

5. Slowly pour hot water into the chamber. You should add only enough water to ensure that the grounds are wet to allow the coffee to bloom.

6. Slowly pour the remaining hot water onto the grounds, then place the plunger on top of the chamber and plunge.

Method 2 — Inverted

1. Insert the plunger into the chamber and turn the Aeropress upside down so that the chamber is at the top.

2. Pull the plunger out to the desired level on the chamber.

3. Add coffee to the chamber, using the measurements described in the traditional method. The ground coffee will sit directly on top of the rubber plunger cap.

4. Boil your water and allow it to cool to between 92°C and 96°C as in the traditional method.

5. Add a small amount of water to the coffee to allow it to bloom. Then add the remaining water.

6. Stir and allow to steep for 1 minute.

7. Insert a paper filter into the filter cap and fit it onto the top of the chamber.

8. Invert the Aeropress and plunge.

FILTER COFFEE

Filter coffee is one of the best brewing methods for enjoying single-origin beans. We have used a Chemex here, but a similar method can be used for other devices like the Hario V60, swiss*gold* and Coava Kone.

TIP
With electric filter equipment, use the ratio of coffee to water outlined here, but follow the instructions on your brewer.

1. Preheat the Chemex by pouring hot water into it and allow it to sit for a couple of minutes before emptying it.

2. Insert a paper filter (you can also use a metal one) into the Chemex.

3. Boil your water and allow it to cool for around 30 seconds so the temperature drops to between 92°C and 96°C.

4. Pour hot water around the filter to ensure that it is fully damp. Empty the residual water.

5. Add freshly ground coffee to the filter — 15g per 250ml of hot water. A coarse filter- or plunger-grind works best.

6. Slowly pour the hot water onto the coffee grounds. You should add only enough water to ensure that the grounds are wet. Leave this to sit until water has finished dripping through the filter. This is called the bloom or pre-infusion.

7. Once the bloom is complete, slowly pour hot water onto the grounds evenly in a circular motion; be sure not to pour too fast, but aim to create 'turbulence' within the coffee. Add water in stages to ensure an even extraction.

8. When you have finished pouring, and the brewing process is complete, lift the filter and dispose of the grounds.

STOVETOP ESPRESSO

1. Using freshly drawn cold water, fill the lower chamber to just below the safety valve.

2. Fill the filter basket with fine-ground, espresso-grind coffee. Gently tap the filter basket to ensure that there are no air pockets or gaps. Ensure the basket is full to the rim. Do not compress the grounds.

3. Put the filter basket into the lower chamber.

4. Remove any loose grounds from the outside rim of the basket, and screw the top chamber on tightly, keeping the pot upright.

5. Place the pot on a medium heat. The coffee needs to have time to infuse properly so do not allow the water to heat too rapidly.

6. Reduce the heat to low if the water starts to boil. When coffee has stopped coming out of the spout in the top chamber (around 8 minutes), remove the stovetop from the heat. Wait for the bubbling to ease before serving.

The filter basket   **The lower chamber**

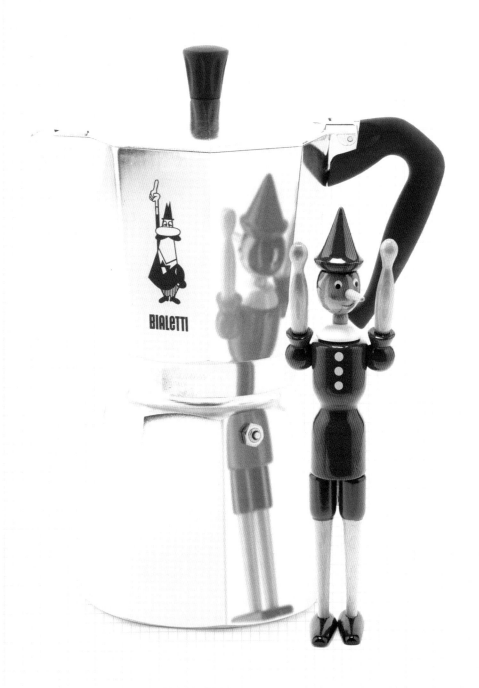

ESPRESSO

Espresso **is the method of extracting the wonderful, volatile oils from fine-ground, roasted coffee using highly pressurised hot water.**

TIP
The methods below will apply to all good espresso equipment, but most particularly to commercial Wega and domestic Rocket espresso machines.

There are three parts to producing an espresso:

1. Extraction (pg. 32)

Extraction is the essence of coffee making — it draws out the coffee's rich, intense flavours.

Extraction should be slow, and the espresso produced thick and viscous, like heavy, dripping oil. A golden brown foam, or crema, should settle on top.

The maximum amount of good coffee that can be extracted from a correctly prepared *group handle* (fitted with a double *filter basket*) of 18g is 60ml. This should take 30 seconds, +/– 5 seconds. If it takes less time, the result will be a watery, bitter espresso with a pale crema. If it takes a lot longer, the result will taste bitter and burnt.

2. Milk texturing (pg. 35) and pouring (pg. 37)

Heated milk should be smooth, creamy and glossy. Heating and pouring techniques will determine the look of the beverage and the texture on the palate.

3. Cleaning (pg. 55)

Routine cleaning of your grinder and espresso machine must be carried out in order to produce a good extraction.

Beans will sweat and leave an oily residue on the grinder's *bean hopper*. Ground coffee left for long periods in the *dosing chamber* will moisten and can become difficult to remove.

Coffee oil will build up on the *group head*, filter baskets and group handles, becoming rancid. Bitter flavours, which many attribute to poorly roasted beans, can actually be a result of dirty equipment.

EXTRACTION

Good extraction is characterised by a 5–10 second delay before any coffee will pour. Heavy droplets will appear and develop into a thick, straight and even pour. The colour will be dark brown or hazelnut, preferably with a reddish reflection.

The pour should be cut off before the colour lightens and the pour begins to curl in.

There are a number of ways to produce a single coffee. According to international best practice, you can:
- use the group handle fitted with a single filter basket to produce one shot of 30ml
- use the group handle fitted with a double filter basket to make two shots (use two cups and extract a maximum of 30ml of espresso into each)
- use the group handle fitted with a double filter basket to produce one 'double shot' of 60ml (extract the espresso into one cup only).

There are three main factors to controlling extraction: dose, tamp and grind.

Dose

The dose is the volume of grounds required in the filter basket to produce the espresso. Wega machine baskets have a reference line that the grounds, once tamped, should just cover for an accurate dose.

There should be about a millimetre between the packed coffee (the *puck*) and the *shower foil*. This allows the hot water to settle over the puck, drawing out as much flavour as possible and allowing room for the grounds to swell.

If there is too little coffee in the basket, hot water will flow through it quickly without extracting the full flavour of the grounds.

Too much coffee in the basket provides excess resistance and makes it difficult for the water to flow through. Without room for the water to settle over the puck, the water will penetrate unevenly and the flavour will not be extracted completely.

TIP

To ensure every coffee tastes as good as it should, the coffee should be freshly ground.

1. Dose the fresh grounds into the basket until full or overflowing. It may take several pulls on the lever of your grinder to do this.

2. Knock the handle on the *tamping mat* to settle the grounds.

3. Evenly distribute the grounds to a level flush with the rim of the basket. You can use your finger or something with a straight edge to do this.

4. Release any excess grounds back into the dosing chamber of your grinder.

Tamp

Tamping is applying firm and even pressure on the dose using a metal implement called a *tamper*. The compressed dose, or puck, offers resistance to the highly pressurised water about to settle on it.

1. Use the wide end of the tamper against the coffee and compress the grounds, using firm, downward pressure to the reference line in the filter basket. Twist the tamper on the puck and lift it off.

2. Reapply the tamper to the surface of the puck and lightly twist it to smooth, or 'polish', the puck's surface.

3. Remove any loose grounds from the *lugs* of the handle.

4. Engage the handle in the group head of the machine and activate the group.

5. Observe the extraction.

Grind

Once you have developed a consistent dosing and tamping technique, you can control the extraction by adjusting the grind setting.

TIP The dry grounds should look like caster sugar — fine yet granular.

TIP If the extraction is too quick, the grind needs to be finer. If the extraction is too slow, the grind needs to be coarsened.

Temperature, humidity and the wearing of the grinder's burrs all affect the accuracy of the grind setting. Adjustments to compensate for these factors may need to be made to control the rate of extraction.

MILK TEXTURING

The most desirable warm milk is smooth and creamy with barely visible bubbles. Good milk should look silky and velvety, like gloss paint.

MILK-TEXTURING TIPS

Cold, full-fat milk produces the best results. Trim milk may be used, but it has a tendency to froth quickly then collapse. Soy milk has a high sugar content, so heats very quickly.

The jug should be about half-full. If you want to make smaller quantities of hot milk, use a smaller jug.

Limit the use of residual milk, as texture and flavour are both compromised by the use of it. If you must use residual milk, make sure it is only a small amount and that it is combined with plenty of fresh milk.

Turn the steam wand on to release condensation before heating the milk.

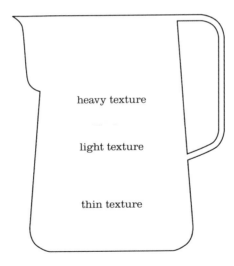

heavy texture

light texture

thin texture

There are three parts to texturing milk. They should be done simultaneously: stretch, swirl and heat.

1/2 full

Stretch

The air must be folded into the milk to stretch it. Place the nozzle just below the surface of the cold milk and turn the steam wand on, releasing its full pressure. As the milk warms and grows, the nozzle should be kept at the top of the milk to continue the stretch.

When the volume of milk has increased by half, the nozzle can remain below the surface of the milk.

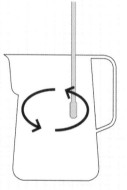

Swirl

Place the steam wand to the side of the jug. This creates a swirling motion in the milk, which keeps the milk nicely blended and smoothes out any bubbles.

3/4 full

Heat

Turn off the steam wand when the milk has reached 60–65°C. You should be able to touch the bottom of the jug but not hold it for any longer than a couple of seconds. If there are any large bubbles, give the jug a heavy knock on the bench to remove them. If there are still a few bubbles, skim off the top couple of millimetres with a spoon. Swirl the jug to reveal a glossy sheen. Now the milk is ready to pour.

MILK POURING

The most important element of milk pouring is to ensure that the milk is nicely blended. Be aware of its texture — heavily textured milk is at the top of the jug, with the lighter-textured milk underneath (see page 35). The longer you let the milk sit, the more it will separate.

There are several methods of controlling texture. Two of them are listed below.

TIP Swirling the milk helps to keep it blended. You should swirl whenever you are not pouring to stop the milk from separating.

Using a spoon

TIP Works best with a bell-shaped jug.

1. Use the spoon like a dam, to hold back the heavy froth. The thinner milk should cut through the dark crema, leaving it relatively undisturbed.

2. As the cup fills, gradually raise the spoon as if you are lifting a gate to release the more heavily textured milk at the top of the jug.

Free pouring

TIP Use a straight-sided jug with a spout.

Splitting the jug

1. Pour off the heavy textured milk at the top into another jug. This is called splitting the jug.

2. Use the remaining milk, which is lighter in texture, to pour your milk-based coffee. From above your cup, and at a slight angle, pour gently into the middle of the dark crema. As the cup fills, bring the milk jug closer to the cup so that it's almost horizontal at the finish. This will release more of the froth at the end of the pour.

3. The remaining milk should be gently mixed in with the heavy milk from the other jug. This combination is now ready for pouring.

For advanced milk pouring, see the section on Latte Art on page 52.

Fig. 1
Using a spoon

Fig. 2
Splitting the jug

KNOW YOUR EQUIPMENT

Rocket R58 Espresso Machine

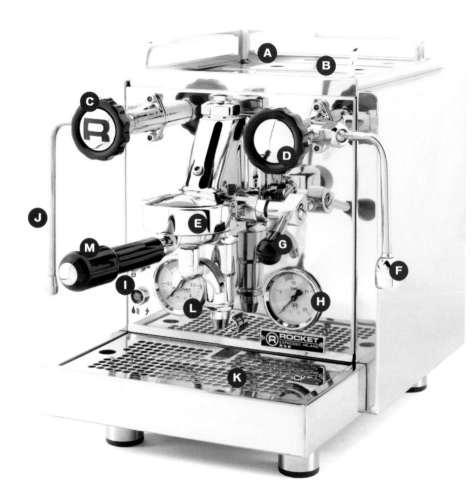

A. Water tank cover	**F.** Hot water wand	**K.** Drip tray
B. Cup tray	**G.** Brew switch	**L.** Steam pressure gauge
C. Steam wand knob	**H.** Pump pressure gauge	**M.** Group handle
D. Hot water tap	**I.** On / off switch	
E. Group head	**J.** Steam wand	

Anfim Best Chrome Grinder

A. Bean hopper
B. Tuning collar

C. Dosing chamber
D. On / off switch

E. Dosing lever
F. Group handle cradle

ESPRESSO COFFEE

How espresso is served varies from café to café.
Factors such as cup volume and shot size play a
role in how the coffee tastes. At L'affare, 40ml
double shots are the norm, as espresso prepared
in this way is richer with a more intense
flavour profile.

The following recipes are based on how we prepare
and serve coffee at our café and should be used as a
guide only.

RISTRETTO

The most concentrated of all espresso beverages, the Ristretto is a
Short Black where the amount of brewed coffee has been 'restricted'.

90ml *demitasse*
20ml restricted double shot

SHORT BLACK / ESPRESSO

This is the base for all espresso beverages.

90ml demitasse
40ml double shot

LONG BLACK

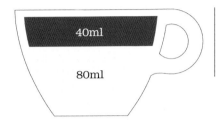

150ml cup
80ml hot water
40ml double shot

The extraction is poured on top of the water so the crema is not disturbed.

AMERICANO

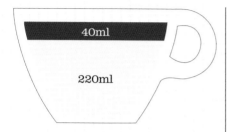

300ml cup
220ml hot water
40ml double shot

The extraction is poured on top of the water so that the crema is not disturbed.

Alternatively, the extraction can be poured directly into the cup, with the hot water served in a jug to the side for your guest to pour themselves.

Americanos can be served with a side of cold milk.

MACCHIATO / LONG MACCHIATO

A Short or Long Black 'marked' with hot milk.

Macchiato

90ml demitasse
40ml double shot
a splash of textured hot milk

Add milk to the espresso with a spoon.

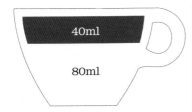

Long Macchiato

150ml cup
80ml hot water
40ml double shot
a splash of textured hot milk

The extraction is poured on top of the water so the crema is not disturbed.

Add milk to the espresso with a spoon.

FLAT WHITE

Flat White drinkers are often the most particular about the way their coffee is prepared.

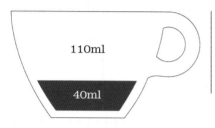

150ml cup
40ml double shot
110ml lightly textured hot milk

Ensure that the milk has very little froth, but is still textured enough to carry without spilling.

CAFFE LATTE

180ml

40ml

220ml glass or cup
40ml double shot
180ml lightly textured hot milk

The texture of the milk in a Caffe Latte can be slightly thicker than that for a Flat White.

BONGO / PICCOLO LATTE

This is a small, intense type of Caffe Latte.

100ml glass
20ml restricted double shot
80ml lightly textured hot milk

It is important that the milk is not too frothy.

CAPPUCCINO

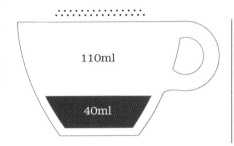

110ml

40ml

150ml cup
40ml double shot
110ml heavily textured hot milk
chocolate powder or cinnamon

Pour milk gently so that the crema remains intact. When the cup is about half-full, 'shake' the heavily textured milk from the jug by rocking it from side to side. Dust with chocolate or cinnamon.

MOCHACCINO

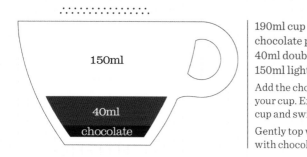

150ml

40ml
chocolate

190ml cup
chocolate powder or syrup to taste
40ml double shot
150ml lightly textured hot milk

Add the chocolate powder or syrup to your cup. Extract your shot into the cup and swirl to combine.

Gently top with milk, then dust with chocolate.

AFFOGATO

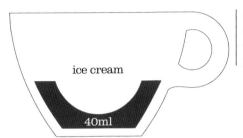

300ml cup
scoop of vanilla ice cream
40ml double shot

Make sure the ice cream is very cold.

Either pour the shot of espresso over the ice cream ...

... or present it on the side for your guest to pour themselves.

LATTE ART

Latte art requires free pouring with a jug that has been split and milk that has a medium texture.

HEART

1. Gently pour the milk into the middle of the dark crema, being careful not to disturb it too much.

2. As the cup fills you should start to 'shake' out the froth from the top of the milk jug by rocking the jug from side to side. Your wrist should stay in the same position. Aim your pour in the same place, too.

3. When the cup is just about full, run the final pour through the centre of the circle to create a heart.

ROSETTA

1. Gently pour the milk into the middle of the dark crema, being careful not to disturb it too much.

3. When the milk reaches the top of the cup, sweep through the pattern by quickly pouring milk up through its centre.

2. When the cup is about half full, begin to rock the milk jug from side to side, slowly moving the jug backwards. A flower pattern will start to appear and fill the cup.

TULIP

1. Tilt the cup and begin your pour in the centre. When the cup is about half-full, begin to rock the milk jug back and forth at the same point to create a circle (similar to starting a heart). Stop.

2. Begin pouring again above the first circle to create another circle, this time pushing into the previous circle to distort it. Stop.

3. Then create a small heart at the top . . .

4. . . . and quickly pour the milk up through the centre of the pattern while lifting the jug to slow and thin out the flow of milk.

TIP
The more circles you create, the more detailed your tulip will be.

CLEANING YOUR ESPRESSO MACHINE

Keeping your machine clean will not only prolong its life, it will also help to improve the quality of the coffee you are able to produce.

After every extraction

After every extraction, empty and rinse the filter basket under the flow of water from the group head.

This serves three purposes:

1. It keeps the group handle clean and free of rancid oils.
2. It heats the handle in preparation for the next extraction.
3. It ensures that the hot water in the group is clean and fresh.

The tools

When cleaning your espresso machine you will require certain tools, all of which can be found in L'affare's Barista's Tool Kit (see page 58).

Rinsing the group head

Remove the filter basket from the group handle and fit the *back-flushing cap*. While the water is flowing, fit the group handle loosely to the group head and rotate the handle back and forth.

Empty the handle of hot water, and check for old grounds as you do this. Repeat until no more grounds appear.

In a café setting, the group head should be rinsed in this way regularly throughout the day. A good rule is after every 10 cups.

You should also regularly scrub the group head with a small plastic brush, like the black-handled one in the Barista's Tool Kit, to dislodge grounds and remove other coffee residue.

Fig. 1
Adding shampoo
to the group

Fig. 2
Activating
water flow

Fig. 3
Final rinse

Back-flushing the group head

The group head should be back-flushed with espresso head cleaning shampoo to ensure it remains clean and in optimal working condition. In a café, this should be done at the end of each day. At home, it is best to back-flush weekly.

Once the group head has been rinsed of grounds using the method on the previous page, add shampoo to the back-flushing cap (in accordance with the manufacturer's instructions), and some boiling water to dissolve it.

Engage the group handle and activate the group head for five seconds, then turn it off. Repeat this five times.

Back-flush the group head using the instructions above (without shampoo this time) to remove any shampoo residue.

You should extract a test shot next time you use the machine to make sure it is completely free from shampoo.

Cleaning the group head and group handles

Prepare a solution using two teaspoons of shampoo dissolved in 500ml of boiling water.

Remove the shower foil and *head seal* from the group head using a ring spanner. Rinse the seal in warm water and put aside.

Using a short-blade screwdriver, unscrew the brass spreader located up inside the group head. Add the brass spreader and shower foil to the solution that you have prepared. Remove the filter basket from the group handle and add this to the solution along with the group handle. Ensure that only the metal end of the handle is covered in the shampoo solution.

After soaking, clean everything to remove any coffee residue, then dry everything thoroughly.

Wipe the group head out with a wet cloth before putting the parts back into place.

Steam wand

Turn the steam wand on before and after use to release condensation and milk residue. Wipe the wand after every use. Do not soak the steam wand in water while it is still attached to the espresso machine as this can cause contaminants to get into the machine's boiler.

If the nozzle of your steam wand is detachable, you can clean it by removing it with an adjustable crescent. Soak it thoroughly in the solution described under 'Cleaning the group head and group-handles'. If the jets get blocked, use a paper-clip to unclog them.

Grinder

Remove the beans from the bean hopper and store them in an airtight container.

Remove the hopper and wash it with warm soapy water to get rid of any oily coffee residue. Thoroughly rinse the hopper and ensure that it is dried properly before it is replaced.

Empty the dosing chamber of grounds and discard them. Use a soft brush, like the red-handled one in the Barista's Tool Kit, to remove all grounds from the throat of the grinder and dosing chamber.

ESPRESSO MENU

Ristretto
- 90ml demitasse
- 20ml restricted double shot

Flat White
- 150ml cup
- 40ml double shot
- 110ml lightly textured hot milk

Short Black / Espresso
- 90ml demitasse
- 40ml double shot

Caffe Latte
- 220ml glass or cup
- 40ml double shot
- 180ml lightly textured hot milk

Long Black
- 150ml cup
- 80ml hot water
- 40ml double shot

Bongo / Piccolo Latte
- 100ml glass
- 20ml restricted double shot
- 80ml lightly textured hot milk

Americano
- 300ml cup
- 220ml hot water
- 40ml double shot

Cappuccino
- 150ml cup
- 40ml double shot
- 110ml heavily textured hot milk

Macchiato
- 90ml demitasse
- 40ml double shot
- a splash of textured hot milk

Mochaccino
- 190ml cup
- Chocolate powder or syrup
- 40ml double shot
- 150ml lightly textured hot milk

Long Macchiato
- 150ml cup
- 80ml hot water
- 40ml double shot
- a splash of textured hot milk

Affogato
- 300ml cup
- scoop of vanilla ice cream
- 40ml double shot

TROUBLESHOOTING

These tips are designed to help fix any problems that occur, providing your espresso machine is running properly in the first place. If a problem persists you should call a technician.

1 Extraction is too fast
- Check the filter basket is not under-dosed.
- Check the grind is not too coarse.

2 Extraction is too slow
- Check the filter basket is not overfull.
- Check the grind is not too fine.
- Check the shower foil is not blocked. It may need to be back-flushed or removed and cleaned.
- Check the spout of the handle is not blocked. If it is dirty with rancid coffee oil, it will need to be soaked in a solution of espresso head cleaning shampoo and water.

3 Water escaping from around the handle
- Check the head seals. If they have dried out, they will need to be replaced.
- Ensure the group handles are kept in place whenever the machine is not in use, as this will help to protect the seals.

4 Espresso is too cold
- Check the cups are warm. You can heat your cups by pouring hot water into them, and then discarding it, before you start your extraction.
- Too much water may have been drawn from the group head. Let the machine rest and limit the amount of water drawn from it between extractions to ensure the machine remains at temperature.

5 Espresso tastes bitter
- Extraction may be too fast. Check the grind is not too coarse. Correct the dose.
- The machine may be dirty. Back-flush and clean the group head. Clean the group handles and filter baskets.

6 Espresso tastes sour
- Extraction may be too slow. Check the grind is not too fine. Correct the dose.

7 Espresso is watery and thin
- Extraction may be too fast. If it is, the crema will be pale. Check the grind is not too coarse. Correct the dose.

8 Espresso is bubbly
- Water from the machine may be too hot. Let some water run from the group head. Try another extraction.
- Coffee could be too fresh.

9 Low or no pressure from steam wand
- May be due to overuse of the group head or hot water tap. Give the machine time to recover pressure.
- The steam wand may be clogged with dry milk. Remove the nozzle, soak it and unclog the jets with a paper-clip.

10 Milk is thin and bubbly
- Ensure the milk is being stretched gradually. If air is introduced too quickly, large bubbles will form.
- Ensure the steam wand is releasing its full pressure and that the jets are not blocked.
- May be due to using reheated milk. Try again with fresh milk.

GLOSSARY

Acidity: term used to explain the pleasant 'brightness' of a coffee.

Arabica: one of the two main species of coffee plant.

Aroma: smell of freshly brewed coffee.

Back-flushing: cleaning an espresso machine by circulating fresh water (often with espresso head cleaning shampoo) through the group head to flush out residual grounds.

Back-flushing cap: blind (unperforated) filter basket used for back-flushing an espresso machine.

Bean hopper: container at the top of the coffee grinder that the roasted whole beans are poured into and held in prior to being ground. Also called a 'hopper'.

Blend: when two or more beans from alternative sources (lots, regions, processing methods, etc.) are combined.

Bloom: releasing the unique aroma and flavour of a coffee by adding a small amount of hot water to dampen coffee grounds.

Body: texture and weight of the coffee in your mouth.

Brass spreader: disperses the pressurised water from the espresso machine through the group head and into the shower foil.

Burr grinder: grinder fitted with a pair of steel discs with cutting edges (teeth) that are designed to grind roasted coffee beans to a desired consistency. Most, if not all, professional baristas use burr grinders.

Cafetière: plunger.

Chemex: hourglass-shaped glass flask that is used to make filter coffee.

Cherry: fruit of the coffee tree.

Crema: golden brown foam that settles on the top of hot coffee (predominantly espresso) once it has been extracted or brewed.

Demitasse: small cup used to serve espresso.

Dose: volume of ground coffee in the filter basket of a group handle.

Dosing chamber: depository underneath the grinder's bean hopper that collects the coffee as it is ground. The dosing chamber has a lever which is used to portion ground coffee into the filter basket.

Dry process: method of extracting the green bean from the cherry of a coffee tree.

Espresso: method of coffee extraction using pressurised hot water to extract oil and flavour from finely ground, roasted coffee.

Filter basket: small, perforated metal basket that fits into a group handle and holds a dose of ground coffee.

Finish: residual feeling and aftertaste of coffee in your mouth.

First crack: distinctive noise in the roasting process that happens when the coffee bean expands and its cell walls break. Occurs between 165°C and 180°C.

Fragrance: smell of roasted, ground coffee prior to brewing.

French press: plunger.

Green bean: one of two seeds from the cherry of a coffee tree.

Group: *see* Group head.

Group handle: device that holds the filter basket and slots into the group head. Also called a 'handle' or 'portafilter'.

Group head: heavy fixed socket(s) of an espresso machine that holds the removable group handle. Also called the 'group'.

Handle: *see* Group handle.

Head seal: rubber seal that fits up inside the group head and holds the shower foil in place.

Honey process: *see* Pulp natural process.

Hopper: see Bean hopper.

Latte art: art of creating a pattern or design when pouring steamed milk into a shot of espresso.

Lugs: parts of the group handle that help to lock it into place within the group head.

One-way valve: valve used in foil coffee packaging that lets gas escape but does not allow oxygen to enter the pack.

Parchment: protective membrane that encases the green bean.

Portafilter: *see* Group handle.

Post-blend: combining beans of various sources after they have been roasted to create a blend.

Press pot: plunger.

Puck: dose in the filter basket once it has been tamped.

Pulp natural process: method of extracting the green bean from the cherry of a coffee tree.

Robusta: one of the two main species of coffee plant.

Second crack: distinctive noise in the roasting process that happens when the coffee bean expands and its cell walls break for a second time. Occurs between 195°C and 220°C.

Semi-washed process: *see* Pulp natural process.

Shot: 30ml serve of espresso coffee.

Shower foil: fitted inside the group head of an espresso machine. Helps to spread hot water evenly across the surface of the puck.

Single origin: beans from one geographical location (e.g. country, region, farm, micro-lot).

Soft brew: term encompassing ways to brew coffee that do not use pressurised hot water like espresso does.

Spout: part of the group handle that delivers espresso to the cup.

Stretch: process of creating foam for milk-based espresso beverages.

Swiss Water Process: process of removing caffeine from green coffee beans using water that is saturated with green coffee extract (GCE).

Tamp: to apply firm and even pressure to the dose.

Tamper: metal tool used to 'tamp' the dose.

Tamping mat: thick rubber mat used to protect the work surface and group handle spouts whilst tamping.

Wet process: method of extracting the green bean from the cherry of a coffee tree.